To Roger Bohue

Darrell Royal

DAN JENKINS'
TEXAS COLLEGE FOOTBALL LEGENDS

Darrell Royal

Dance With Who Brung Ya

By Mike Jones

Edited by
Dan Jenkins

SPORTS

IN ASSOCIATION WITH THE

Fort Worth Star-Telegram

WESLEY R. TURNER, President and Publisher
MICHAEL BLACKMON, Vice President, Editorial Director
JACK B. TINSLEY, Vice President, Community Affairs
JIM WITT, Vice President, Executive Editor
KEVIN DALE, Managing Editor

Acknowledgements

All chapters in the "Ten to Remember" section are reprinted
by permission of the *Fort Worth Star-Telegram*. Copyright © 1958, 1962, 1963, 1964,
1965, 1969, 1970 and 1976 by the *Fort Worth Star-Telegram*. All rights reserved.

Designed by Daniel J. Janke and Richard Epps

ISBN 1-57028-164-5
ISBN (Leatherbound Edition) 1-57028-173-4

Published by

Masters Press
2647 Waterfront Parkway, East Drive
Indianapolis, Indiana 46214
317-298-5706

For other sports publications in the Masters Press library,
call toll-free 1-800-722-2677 or contact our web site at www.masterspress.com

CONTENTS

FOREWORD

Royal & Jenkins: A Pair of Champions

It's the sweetest sight I can imagine. A sun-kissed, fall Saturday afternoon sitting next to my dad at an Oklahoma football game, watching the Sooners line up in their powerful Wishbone offense. I couldn't conceive of another way to run an offense.

Think of my distress when I learned that credit for the offense had to go to a Longhorn, a dreaded rival from the University of Texas. But as I grew to love college football, it was obvious that I had to love Darrell Royal, just a little. In 1957, a 32-year-old Royal took over a floundering Texas program. The improvement was immediate and prolonged.

Royal spent the next 20 years marching through college football. He retired as the winningest coach in Southwest Conference history in 1976, his legendary status intact.

He was an immediate choice to be included in the Dan Jenkins' Texas College Football Legends series. The series will include profiles of a dozen players and coaches who have shaped college football in a state that has been producing Saturday afternoon thrills for decades.

Why Royal? Sixteen bowl games, an overall record of 167-47-5, 11 SWC titles won or shared, a number of innovations (remember the Wishbone). Then there's the matter of five national championships. Through it all, Royal took the high road.

As Fort Worth Star-Telegram sportswriter Whit Canning wrote in a 1995 historical piece: "More than the numbers, however, there was the national image of excellence — and class — that cloaked Royal's teams like the famous burnt-orange jerseys they wore.

"In moments of triumph, the Longhorns proved to be admirable and popular heroes — never belittling those they had vanquished. And with his engaging personality and down-home humor — source of the famed 'Royalisms' — their coach slowly evolved into a national icon."

It's not surprising that Royal would rise to the top of his profession. He was born into a poor Oklahoma family. His mother died when he was 4 months old. His father found work where he could, ending up in California. Royal paid $10 for a ride back to Hollis after receiving a letter from the high school football coach. He worked for everything that came his way.

He took that work ethic into college football. He changed the face of coaching in the 1950's with impeccable organization and aggressive recruiting.

"I was 32 years old and very naive," Royal told Canning in 1995. "I was also aggressive and highly competitive and couldn't wait to get to work. And I kept pinching myself, wondering how I had managed to become the head coach at a great place like the University of Texas."

That wide-eyed love of football is something Royal shares with the namesake of this series. Dan Jenkins is synonymous with football in Texas. He grew up in Fort Worth, watching his beloved TCU Horned Frogs. When he decided to turn his attention to chronicling those Saturday afternoon feats, the sports world became a better place.

Southwest Conference football spoke to Jenkins, and he translated for the rest of us. This project is a labor of love, even if Royal's record against TCU was 15-5.

Kevin Dale
Managing Editor
The Fort Worth Star-Telegram

St. Darrell

By Dan Jenkins

Let's get something straight right away. Darrell K Royal of the University of Texas, as great a college football coach as ever danced with what brung him, won five national championships with the burnt orange Longhorns. Five, I said. Not three.

Attention University of Texas sports information department. Three is wrong. Why only three? Divorce three, Marry five.

I figure this is the nicest thing I can do for Darrell, a guy who was my best friend and best source among coaches in all the years that my typewriter carried me around the sport. Correct the record.

Put him up there where he belongs. Up there with the elite dozen coaches who have grabbed the most No. 1 titles in the whole 128-year history of the college game.

Where do I get the number five?

Oh, just right out of something called the *Official NCAA Football Record Book*, that's all. It's published annually, if you're curious.

The book lists every team in every season that's ever been awarded any kind of national title — and by who, what, and which selector. Not just the wire services, and who says they're the only ones that count, anyhow?

The titles are all mythical. Which is not to say that boosters and old grads don't offer them engagement rings and take them home to meet mother.

So here are Royal's five national championship teams along with the selectors and a few of the gladiators that were identified with them:

President Lyndon Johnson congratulates Texas coach Darrell Royal following the Longhorns' 1963 national championship.

1961 (10-1) — Sagarin System (USA Today now) ... James Saxton. Don Talbert.

1963 (11-0) — AP, UPI, Football Writers, Helms, Hall of Fame, Dunkel System, Litkenhous System, Williamson System, Sagarin System, Football News, Berryman System, Poling System, Football Research, National Championship Foundation ... Duke Carlisle, Tommy Ford, Tommy Nobis, Scott Appleton.

1968 (9-1-1) — Football News, Sagarin System, Matthews System ... Chris Gilbert, James Street, Loyd Wainscott.

1969 (11-0) — AP, UPI, Football Writers, Football News, Helms, Dunkel System, Litkenhous System, Football Research, Berryman System, Hall of Fame, Poling System, Sagarin System, National Championship Foundation, Football Analysis System ... James Street, Steve Worster, Cotton Speyrer, Bob McKay, Glen Halsell, Bobby Wuensch.

1970 (10-1) — UPI, Hall of Fame, Litkenhous System, Berryman System, Football Analysis System ... Steve Worster, Eddie Phillip, Cotton Speyrer, Scott Henderson, Bill Atessis.

And as Bear Bryant once said, "You only need to win one in a season, then your people can play like they won 'em all."

You may wonder where this ranks St. Darrell, as he was known to the more passionate Longhorn followers, among the immortals. According to my favorite reference work, the *Official NCAA Football Record Book*, here are the all-time top dozen coaches where No. 1 trinkets are concerned:

1. *Bear Bryant, Alabama* 10
2. *Howard Jones, USC, Iowa, Yale* 9
   Woody Hayes, Ohio State 9
4. *Tom Osborne, Nebraska* 8
5. *Barry Switzer, Oklahoma* 7
   Bobby Bowden, Florida State 7

(Left to right) Dan Jenkins, Royal and a pair of sports writers visit with actress Jill St. John in New York in 1959.

Aside from those No. 1 teams, Darrell turned out a few other squads that you wouldn't leave sitting on the curb. In six other seasons — '59, '62, '64, '72, '73 and '75 — his Longhorns finished in the nation's Top Ten. And in four other seasons — '57, '60, '71 and '74 — they wound up in the Top 20.

In Darrell's twenty years as head coach of the Longhorns, therefore, it works out that there were only five seasons when he *did not* produce a Top 20 team. Horrors. A man could get fired for such an oversight today, attention spans and loyalties being what they've become.

It further behooves me to mention that since polls began in 1924 Darrell is on a rather exclusive list of guys who both played on a national championship team in college and later coached one. Before Royal did all those wonderful things in Austin, he all-American quarterbacked the unblemished '49 Oklahoma Sooners, which grabbed a No. 1 and may have been Bud Wilkinson's most powerful team.

In any event, Royal is joined in the club by only eight others. They happen to be: Harry Stuhldreher (Notre Dame, Wisconsin), Frank Leahy (Notre Dame), Bear Bryant (Alabama), Bud Wilkinson (Minnesota, Oklahoma), Bump Elliott (Michigan), Jim Owens (Oklahoma,

Washington), Jackie Sherrill (Alabama, Pitt), and Jimmy Johnson (Arkansas, Miami).

I could keep on talking numbers and lists for St. Darrell. Mention his 11 Southwest Conference titles, his 16 bowl teams, his 26 all-Americans that wore the burnt orange. The 25 different Saturdays over the years that his teams had to carry the No. 1 burden of the weekly polls into a stadium, and the 20 times they won those games.

But Darrell wasn't really about numbers. More than anything else, I think, he was about making an athlete get the best out of himself.

I'll always remember one of those signs he put up on the dressing room wall. He'd have a different one each season. The kids were supposed to glance at it every time they walked out the door for a workout or a game. For this particular sign, many of them stopped and scratched their heads, and I guess it was James Street, the undefeated quarterback, who nudged me one day and said with a grin, "If you can figure that thing out, let me know."

The sign said: WHAT I GAVE I KEPT. WHAT I KEPT I LOST.

Later, I said to Darrell, "Don't you think that's a little deep for them?"

He said, "Well, I guess I could just put one up that says BEAT A&M."

Most of the collectible "Royalisms" will be recanted elsewhere in this tribute. The ones I most often recall were the offhanded, game-face remarks.

"Don't matter what they throw at us," he'd say, slipping on the game-face, "only angry people win football games."

Strolling with him up there in the Ozarks before the Big Shootout in '69, he started getting the game-face on a day early, at a workout.

"Arkansas," he said, as he might have said the word cockroach. "What the hell is it good for? All they do is sell jams and jelly by the side of the road."

He won't forget the green socks — and neither will I.

The year was '63. I had made the pre-season college football forecast for *Sports Illustrated* and picked Texas to be No. 1. Most of the other "authorities" went with USC, Alabama, Oklahoma, Ole Miss, but I thought the Longhorns had a genuine shot — largely because of their coach.

Texas took over the top spot the fourth week when it stunned Oklahoma, 28 to 7. The Longhorns then held it in excruciating battles against Arkansas (17-13), Rice (10-6), and SMU (17-12). They were 7-0 going into the tough Baylor game, and I was in prayer.

Obviously, if Texas could win the national championship, I would be hoisted on shoulders and carried down

Royal and pro golfer Lee Trevino share a laugh during a golf outing in Austin, Tex.

Left, Royal receives a No. 1 plaque by President Richard Nixon after the Longhorns defeated Arkansas in "The Game of the Century" in 1969. Above, Royal visits with a trio of Texas fans, (left to right) W.L. Todd, Bob Hope and Arnold Palmer.

the halls of *Sports Illustrated* and deemed a clairvoyant.

Somewhere along the way, however, and within the hallowed pages of the magazine, I had quoted Royal talking about his opponents, insinuating that they were of a inferior breed to Longhorns, intellectually and socially. Another game-face deal.

I'd quoted him saying something on the order of, "You know the guy in the blue serge suit with his green socks rolled down didn't go to Texas."

Well, the green and gold Baylor Bears not only showed up in Austin on Nov. 9, 1963, with a 6-1 record, with Don Trull and Lawrence Elkins — the best passing combo in the land — but with 20,000 fans waving long green socks in the air.

I was up in the Memorial Stadium press box that day

when I saw those green socks, and my first thought was that Darrell would have his game-face on for me, not Baylor.

This was the game where Duke Carlisle made the great game-saving interception, of course, and Texas won a 7-0 thriller, and went on to become unanimous national champion.

More importantly, where a purely unbiased sportswriter was concerned, I don't know that I've ever rooted as hard for one specific team to win a football game as I did for the Longhorns that Saturday.

If 10 years passed before Darrell and I might run into each other again, I think I know one of the subjects that would come up.

The day we both survived the green socks.

14 TEXAS   0   02:26
4 DOWN   2 TO GO   2 TO 4   BALL 0

REPUBLIC NATIONAL

"A Longhorn Icon"

CHAPTER ONE

More Than a Coach

A Poor Oklahoma Boy Travels to the Top of the College Football World and Builds an Unforgettable Legacy

The long day caught up with Darrell Royal late that night. On a curve approaching an old concrete bridge on a lonely stretch of rural Oklahoma highway outside of Hollis, Royal fell asleep at the wheel of his pre-World War II Chevy.

Then a freshman at the University of Oklahoma, he and the rest of the Sooner football team had been given a few days off for the holidays. Oklahoma was preparing for the first Gator Bowl game in 1946 against North Carolina State.

Darrell was making a quick trip home to rejoin his young family for Christmas Day. His wife had been restricted from traveling during the latter days of her pregnancy. Edith, expecting their second child, was waiting at home in Norman with their young daughter, Marian.

After spending some time with his dad and brothers, Darrell had driven out of town to visit with some friends. On the way home, he dozed off.

As it left the farm-to-market road, Royal's car demolished one side of the bridge railing and was airborne. The Chevy wiped out the tops of two aged cottonwoods before it plunged downward and tumbled into the field that ran alongside the creek bottom.

"I was on the ground on the bank before I knew what was happening," Royal remembered more than 50 years later. "The car was demolished, but I was pitched out. The car was rolling over and over and the driver's side door was open. I saw the door disappear into the mud. That door blowing open was the only way I lived."

Stunned, Royal checked himself over and did not find any broken bones, only a scratch on his face. Steam hissed out of the mangled radiator. Royal's first thought was to find something in which to save the antifreeze leaking into the soil.

"Antifreeze was important then because it was hard to get during the war," Royal said. "I don't remember whether it was readily available again at the time, but that was my first thought — to try and save as much of that antifreeze as I could."

A farmer who lived nearby — and whose mud Royal was now covered in — soon drove up on his tractor in a huff. He had been awakened from a snug winter's nap upon hearing the commotion that echoed through the still December night.

"The first question he asked was, 'Did you hit my bull?' He didn't ask if I was hurt, or if there was anyone else in the car. All he was interested in was his bull. I told him I hadn't hit his bull, but I did ask him if he had a bucket so we could catch what was left of my antifreeze."

Whether or not Royal saved any of that once-precious green liquid, he cannot remember. Presumably, the farmer's prized bull lived a long life and sired many offspring. And fate, destiny or the good Lord — take your pick — had more than a few things yet in mind for the young man with the quick mind, strong body and startling good looks.

"The strangest thing," Royal remembers. "Before the wreck, I used to dream that I was tumbling — in danger — and then everything is all right. I never had that dream after the wreck."

Amazingly, Royal played in the Sooners' 34-13 upset victory in the Gator Bowl a week after surviving the au-

Royal and Edith (left) visit with Alfred Hitchcock (middle) and Veronique and Gregory Peck at Universal Studios in 1964.

to accident. He finished his Oklahoma playing career three years later as an all-American quarterback on an undefeated team that finished the season ranked No. 1 in the nation in 1949. He is still revered as one of the most versatile players in Sooner football history, despite never playing at a weight of more than 170 pounds.

Royal eventually went on to coach at the University of Texas, where he became one of the most legendary football coaches of the modern era — retiring suddenly in 1976 at the relatively young age of 52 after 20 seasons. During his tenure, the Longhorns won five national championships, 11 Southwest Conference titles and played in 16 bowl games while compiling a 167-45-5 record.

Royal coached 77 all-SWC players and 26 all-Americans at Texas. In 23 years as a head coach, his teams never had a losing season.

After 18 years as athletic director at Texas, he retired in 1978 and continues to work on selected projects as a special assistant to the university president. He also serves as chairman of the Board of Governors of the Barton Creek development — the unique residential development in the hills of West Austin.

"As chairman of the board, Darrell commands the same amount of respect he did when he was coaching the football team," said former player Jim Bob Moffett (1959-60), whose giant world-wide natural resource development company owned the Barton Creek complex until 1997.

"It's amazing. We don't ever get any complaints, because Darrell works it out. If those guys who run that club — whether it's the 19th hole or the locker room or the golf course — if they can satisfy Coach Royal, most of the members are going to be happy.

"Darrell has that same ability today that he had back when he was on the field. All he has to do is walk into the area and everybody straightens up their act. He has a great ability to command respect just by his presence. And he's been able to pull that off ever since I've known him."

In fact, Moffett said he organized and continues to run his international corporation based on principles he learned from his former coach, with whom he has continued to consult for common-sense business advice for more than 30 years.

Emerging from the swirl of the Dust Bowl that ravaged the Midwest during the early years of The Depression in the 1930's, Royal survived a difficult childhood to become not only a coaching legend and an icon in his adopted state of Texas, but to call as friend a President of the United States, actors, authors, poets, musicians and entertainers of all ilk while maintaining an everlasting kinship with the everyman — regardless, as he is fond of saying, of a person's "rank and smell."

The late former President Lyndon B. Johnson, who developed a fast friendship with Royal after retiring from office, once wrote, "I am not a football fan, but I am a fan of people, and I am a Darrell Royal fan because he is the rarest of human beings."

Royal did not retire from coaching in 1976 to sit on the couch. Among other pursuits, he has committed himself to support and nurture his beloved community of Austin, much as Midwestern farmers once replanted thousands of acres of Great Plains grasslands to help prevent the reoccurrence of the massive erosion that drove families from their homes and family farms in the early 30's.

As the organizer, mover and shaker behind the annual Ben Willie Darrell East Austin Youth Classic golf tournament — with professional golfer and Austin native Ben Crenshaw and legendary country music

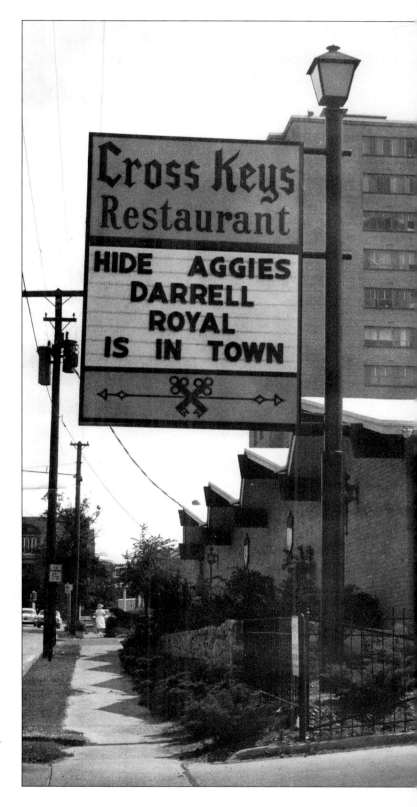

17

Royal and frequent golf partner Frank Broyles, of Arkansas, once played 65 holes of golf in one day.

star Willie Nelson — Royal is responsible for pumping approximately half a million dollars annually into East Austin. These grants benefit the rainbow of youth in the historic and multi-racial section of the city that lies east of the Capitol dome and north of the Colorado River.

"The 20 or so years since I have quit coaching have gone by fast, much faster than I realized they would," said Royal who at a firm and fit 73 years old plays golf almost every day and works out every morning at the Barton Creek Country Club spa.

"I've been asked what I do with my time, but really and truly my calendar is full. I've spent very few days of boredom. I do what I want to do. I don't necessarily have

to do anything anymore, but my calendar is full — full of things I want to do."

In August 1996, the university announced plans to add Royal's name to Memorial Stadium, henceforth known as the Darrell K Royal-Texas Memorial Stadium, which is now undergoing a massive facelift and expansion as part of what may eventually be a $40 million capital improvement project that will include a new track and soccer stadium and women's softball field, among other things.

"The main idea behind adding Darrell's name to the stadium was to honor a man who has been connected with the university for 40 years and who had more to do with athletics at Texas than anyone else in its history," said Mack Rankin — a longtime friend of Royal's, a 1950 UT graduate and the chairman of the Longhorn Legacy Foundation that is coordinating private donations for the project.

"It is the climax to a great career," Rankin said. "The focal point is to honor Darrell and to give added meaning to the stadium and the man who really built it. People talked about old Yankee Stadium as the House that Ruth Built. They talked about the Cotton Bowl as the House that Doak Built. And certainly if we'd kept going like we were when Darrell came to Texas in 1956, we'd still be playing in a 36,000-seat stadium."

The decision to add Royal's name to the stadium came out of a meeting at Bauer House, the official residence of the system chancellor. Present that night were members of the UT administration, the Board of Regents, the Athletics Council, members of the Longhorn Advisory Council and selected others involved for the previous four years in the planning of Memorial Stadium expansion — the first since 1977.

When a consensus was instantly reached that adding Royal's name was a fitting honor and might prove to be a boon in raising the necessary millions of dollars in private donations, Chancellor William H. Cunningham, then-UT president Robert M. Berdahl and Regents chairman Bernard Rapaport were delegated to broach the idea to Royal — who in the past had been known to lend his support to any fund-raising project, but who had always shunned direct involvement in asking for donations of any kind.

"That kind of thing has always been uncomfortable for me to do and the people with the university know that," Royal said. "I've always enjoyed doing anything the university asked me to do, and I've never done anything that I considered boring or that was hard for me to do. But I have not gone and asked for money.

"There have been people who have voluntarily given because they knew we had drives going and they let me know they had done it, but I don't ask for it."

So when he got the call one day that Cunningham, Berdahl and Rapaport wanted to come to his house to talk to him, Royal was puzzled.

"First of all, I wondered what I had done," Royal said. "I told Edith I had no idea what they could want. But I knew it must be important or they wouldn't have wanted to come to the house."

When they presented the proposal, the usually glib Royal was at a loss to respond. Edith said Darrell just sat there.

"He was really beside himself," she said.

After an embarrassing silence, Cunningham nervously said that if Royal didn't approve, they would shelve the idea.

A TRIO OF GREAT TEXANS: Lady Bird Johnson (middle) with Edith and Darrell Royal.

Mel Allen (middle) introduces Royal and Oklahoma coach Bud Wilkinson at a Look gathering in New York in 1959.

"I said, 'My gosh, is that what you're waiting on?' Me to tell you it's all right?" Royal said. "When I say I was struck dumb, I'm not lying."

Edith said the gesture has touched Darrell more than most people realize.

"He never dreamed something like that would happen to him," she said. "It's been very fulfilling for him."

Indeed, few are so honored during a lifetime.

"It's a shame that that's the way most of the rules are written," Royal said. "How is a guy to know? He gets no pleasure out of it.

"They had the building at the end of the stadium (the Neuhaus-Royal Athletic Complex) with my name on it, but I had no idea they would ever name anything else after me. Any coach who has a facility where he coached for many years named after him would feel the highest form of flattery. But I never dreamed. ..."

Some members of the Austin community bristled at the announcement of the name change, feeling that to add Royal's name cast a shadow over the stadium that was first dedicated in 1924 as a memorial to those heroic Texas veterans who lost their lives on the field of battle in World War I. That was certainly is not the intent, said Franklin W. Denius, a prominent Austin attorney who, as a teenager storming the beaches of Normandy on D-Day in June 1944, became one of the most decorated soldiers of World War II.

Denius chairs the Longhorn Advisory Council capital funding committee and also served as coordinator of a veterans committee that organized a re-dedication of the stadium as a veterans' memorial in the fall of 1997.

"We've worked hard to revitalize the recognition of the stadium as a memorial," Denius said. "But we also wanted to pay tribute to Darrell Royal for the great leadership he provided not only as a football coach, but as an athletic director. And the quality of his loyalty has to go in there, too — paralleling equally the recognition of Darrell's ability to motivate young people to accomplish the best that they can."

Those principles Royal once taught of preparation, dedication to a task and organization — he's the guy who said repeatedly that luck is when preparation meets opportunity — still live in many of his former players. Royal's name will live on not only in the edifice of an athletic complex, but in the lives of those who have been touched by association.

"The fundamental things he taught us — not only about how to play the game of football — but the principles of how to conduct ourselves and carry on our business have helped me to do my job better in my life away from playing," said Tommy Nobis, the former Longhorn all-American linebacker of the mid-1960's, five-time NFL Pro Bowl selection and current director of player development for the Atlanta Falcons.

"There are a lot of guys out there who are successful because he pushed us and worked us so hard. And you did it the coach's way. There was no in-between about how you were going to act on or off the field as a Texas Longhorn."

For Austin banker James Saxton, star running back of the "Flip-Flop" offense in the early 1960's, the relationship went beyond coach-player.

"To me, Coach Royal was like a father," Saxton said. "He gave me the opportunity to talk to him when I needed to. I felt comfortable with him. And he talked to me when he felt like he needed to.

"That was very unique, because I didn't have a dad. My mother and father divorced when I was very small, so he was like a father to me more than anybody. There just aren't many Darrell Royals in this world."

Certainly there have been few like him in the coaching profession.

"Darrell was a great coach," said former University of Arkansas coach Frank Broyles, who remains the Razorbacks' athletic director after a long and stellar coaching career that paralleled that of his long-time friend, foe and marathon golfing partner. (Royal and Broyles once played 91 holes in a day.)

"I look at the four or five great coaches in my era and I think that Darrell had the best combination of football knowledge ... and down-to-earth leadership without any manipulation. The legacy he left in the profession was not only his winning record but his integrity. And suc-

Former Notre Dame coach Frank Leahy shares strategy with Royal in New York in 1970.

cess never changed him."

Some will feel the Royal legacy without having ever met the man or perhaps ever knowing of his accomplishments on the playing or coaching field.

Richard Slaughter, the administrator of the Austin Community Foundation that has distributed approximately $3.5 million raised by the Ben Willie Darrell tournament, says: "There has been a lot of breadth and depth to where the money raised by this golf tournament has gone. Five years ago we were struggling to make $1 million in grants and they come to us with another half a million a year? We had to grow up in a hurry. We literally had grant requests written on brown paper.

"But what this golf tournament also has done is give us all sorts of new friends who had never heard of us in East Austin — like someone just raised the window-shade and said, 'Look out of the other side of your house, because you've got folks living over here, too.'"

Royal moved his and Willie's charity bash from Houston in 1991 to focus on East Austin after serving untold beneficiaries — such as the Galveston Boys Club — in 20 previous years. The tournament's millions have provided funding for such varied things as computers for schools, summer baseball and basketball leagues, after-school care programs, arts programs in elementary schools and revitalization of playgrounds. The one near Allison Elementary School on Vargas Road was brought back to life through a $30,000 grant from the Foundation in partnership with the Austin Independent School District, Austin's Parks and Recreation Department, local parents and other interested neighborhood parties.

"And the big kids now respect that playground because they know it belongs to their little brothers and sisters and they know their parents helped put it there," Slaughter said. "So many kids have benefited from Coach Royal's golf tournament. We have one East Austin youth league that services 1,200 youngsters. Some of the benefits have been bricks and mortar like that playground. But you can't see all the benefits on the surface. It's inside the kids."

Royal and Edith enjoy a backstage meeting with the Pecks and Doris Day in Hollywood.

Ben Crenshaw, Willie Nelson (middle) and Royal at the 1997 Ben Willie Darrell Golf Tournament.

The benefits of having been a part of Edith and Darrell Royal's life are very real to songwriter-entertainer Larry Gatlin, one of many who have felt the genuine love and concern of a couple who have been life partners for more than 50 years.

"I believe I would be dead if not for Darrell and Edith, I really do," Gatlin said. "My wife, Janice, and my brother, Steve, had both confronted me about my alcoholism and drug addiction and I blew them off. It wasn't that I didn't love them, I just had to have somebody from outside the family circle to grab me by the collar.

"Well, Edith and Darrell knew and they prayed about it and finally Darrell had the courage to say to me one night, 'You know, Larry, you are my friend and I love you. But you are messed up. You need help.'

"We made a deal that if I couldn't do it on my own, I'd go get help. And Darrell had a place he wanted to take me when it was time and I realized I could not get rid of my addictions by myself. He met me in Fort Worth and flew out with me to the treatment center and stayed there with me."

Gatlin has been sober since Dec. 9, 1984.

"I love Darrell and Edith," Gatlin said. "They are

like my family. I'm a little guy and not a bad-ass by any means. But anyone wants to hurt Darrell or Edith, they are going to have to come through me and they ain't gonna like it. They better bring a sack lunch and a flashlight, because they're gonna get hungry and it's gonna get dark."

Songwriter, entertainer and cowboy poet Red Stegall echoes the devotion many feel. Stegall has known Royal since the first Dripping Springs Reunion in 1974. He and his wife, Gail, were married in the Royals' back yard.

"I have met a lot of people in my life," noted Stegall, the poet laureate of Texas. "But I have never met anyone as magnetic as Darrell. I don't know how to explain it other than to say that once you become part of his world, you don't ever want to leave it."

Austin sporting goods dealer Rooster Andrews, who first gained fame as the all-American water boy, has shared with the Royals the triumph and tragedy of a friendship of more than 40 years. Within nine months of 1972, the former neighbors shared the unfortunate deaths of their daughters, who both died in their 20's.

"Let me tell you something about Darrell," Andrews said. "There has been a time or two when something would happen that you'd think Darrell might come by, but he'd be busy or out of town or something.

"But you got your country ass in trouble, he was the first guy at your doorstep. He'd know you were in trouble. And I tell you, there was a time or two he knew I was in trouble before I knew it myself. And he was there.

"He'd say, 'Look, I'm just telling you. And I want you to be brave.' He did things no one else would dare do. They just wouldn't take the risk. But Darrell sure would."

It's easier to find someone who has never heard of Darrell Royal than a person who really knows him and has no genuine feeling for him. In truth, however, there is at least one who has held a grudge against the man for more than 30 years — Texas A&M football coach R.C. Slocum.

It was the fall of 1962. Royal by now had built his program into a national power, though the Longhorns were a season away from their first of five national championships. Slocum was a senior at Orange High School. He

was also a nominee for most-handsome boy in his class, and the OHS yearbook sponsors had succeeded in getting Royal to agree to pick the most handsome boy and most beautiful girl from each of the three classes.

You guessed it. Royal — or whoever actually made the choices — somehow failed to recognize the charming good looks of one R.C. Slocum. Somebody else was picked most handsome boy in the senior class.

"I once told him that I had held a grudge against him for a long time and that I thought he used very poor judgment in his selection," Slocum said laughing.

"But at the time as a boy growing up and playing football in the state of Texas, Darrell Royal was THE coach. He epitomized football in this state for guys my age."

Royal later provided inspiration for Slocum, who came from humble origins as Royal did. Slocum also shined shoes and worked at any job he could find to help supplement his family's income.

"I remember reading or hearing a story once where Darrell talked about getting his first new pair of shoes. He would walk around rocks to avoid scuffing the soles," Slocum recalled. "I think a lot of guys like myself that grew up poor and worked while they were going to school identified with that.

"I think Darrell has always remembered where he came from. Some people who come from those backgrounds and work themselves out of it — all of the sudden you think they grew up in a country club. They try to put on airs of being something they're not. The one thing that stands out most in my mind about him is that he cares about and respects people of all backgrounds. He's been around Presidents, but he has lived part of his life with the common man and he never lost touch with the guy on the street. That has impressed me about him more than anything else.

"But I've always thought that his greatest legacy to coaching was that he proved you can win without being a jerk. Some guys you have to give credit to because they've won, but they're a pain in the butt to be around. I think a thing like Darrell's charity golf tournament is really one of the greatest tributes to a man you can have

In 1996, Memorial Stadium was renamed Darrell K Royal-Texas Memorial Stadium.

— he's got all those people playing in that tournament because they care about the guy.

"A lot of coaches, once they're out of the profession, their friends shrink up in a hurry. But I think Darrell's friends have grown more and more over the years because of the kind of person he is."

Former Dallas Cowboys' all-pro quarterback Roger Staubach, whose Navy team lost to Royal's Longhorns in the 1964 Cotton Bowl, says that Royal reminds him of former Cowboys' coach Tom Landry.

"They are different type people, but their personali-

ties as coaches are similar," Staubach said. "Both are good people who have a lot of respect from their former players and a history of consistently winning. And that's not an accident when you do it for as long a period of time as they did.

"Darrell is just a first-class guy ... his former players love him. Everybody who played for Darrell Royal that I've known just can't say enough about what he meant to the program at Texas. Being head of a real estate firm in Dallas with a lot of Longhorn fans in the company, to them Darrell Royal is still the benchmark for Texas football."

CHAPTER TWO

Hollis, Okla.

A Teenager's Trip to California
and a Return to Oklahoma to Fulfill a Destiny

The soon-to-be blazing sun had yet to break the California horizon to the east when the 15-year-old boy climbed into the cab of the one-armed man's pickup.

He carried with him only a box that had once held a table-top Victrola record player with the hand crank. Into the box, he had crammed all his worldly possessions. He set the makeshift travel valise down on the seat beside him — out of the way of the shifting rod that stuck up through the pickup's floorboard but reassuringly close to his left leg. Throughout the 1,500-mile journey that would put him back in his hometown of Hollis, Oklahoma, in time for the start of his high school sophomore year, Darrell Royal never let that box out of his sight.

Besides a small stash of hard-earned cash, the only thing of value the young man carried was a much-read and refolded letter from his high school football coach, Dean Wild, who had just been promoted from assistant coach. Wild — well-aware that Darrell was the best athlete in town — had written Royal that if he wanted to come home and go back to high school in Hollis, he could have a job at the local Ford dealership before and after school, making $5 a week.

"That letter was an encouragement to me," said Royal, who had come west that spring in search of work with his father, his stepmother and Glenn, one of his three older brothers. "And understand, I didn't need much encouragement to leave California. Just a little. And that letter was enough.

Royal was a star quarterback at Hollis High in Oklahoma.

"That California segment of my life is still strong in my memory, where some aren't. I'm not saying we had it as bad as the blacks or Hispanics. But when they called us 'Okie' out there, it just had a real bad ring to it. It was like people out there hated us just because we wanted an honest job."

From his overalls, the teenager took a $10 bill and handed it to the man, the agreed-upon price for a journey halfway across the United States. A former Royal family friend who now ran a used-car lot in Bakersfield, Calif., had helped the young man line up the ride through an agency that arranged such rendezvous between those with transportation looking for gas money and the thousands of hard-working, Americans afoot. In August of 1940, they were the ones who streamed back and forth across a country still trying to emerge from the grips of the nationwide economic disaster of the 1930's called The Great Depression.

Shortly after the stock market crash of 1929 — the event that sounded the starting gun for more than a decade of economic woes in America — the nation's breadbasket turned to burnt toast.

Man had taken plow to the heart of the nation's grasslands during the early years of World War I, land that a century before supported massive herds of buffalo. Open range that had been home to scattered herds of cattle in the early 20th century were turned over and planted in wheat as part of the war effort and beyond.

Poor land management during the 1920's was followed by a disastrous drought that lasted several years during the early 1930's over a section of the country that embraced the panhandles of Texas and Oklahoma, southwestern Kansas, southeastern Colorado and northeastern New

A young Darrell Royal, age 3, at home in Hollis, Okla.

Mexico. Spring winds came and lifted exposed, parched topsoil no longer held by the roots of native grasses into boiling storms that were called Black Blizzards and gave the region the designation as the Dust Bowl.

Such a celebrated storm it was that whisked Dorothy out of Kansas. But to a cast of thousands, California became their Land of Oz.

John Steinbeck dramatized the plight of the suddenly displaced Midwesterners in a famous passage from his classic 1939 novel, *The Grapes of Wrath*:

"And then the dispossessed were drawn west from Kansas, Oklahoma, Texas, New Mexico, from Nevada and Arkansas; families, tribes, dusted out, tractored out. Carloads, caravans, homeless and hungry; twenty thousand and fifty thousand and a hundred thousand and two hundred thousand. They streamed over the mountains, hungry and restless — restless as ants, scurrying to find work to do — to lift, to push, to pull, to pick, to cut — anything, any burden to bear, for food. The kids are hungry. We got no place to live. Like ants scurrying for work, for food, and most of all for land."

Royal and others who remember the period that shaped the generation of our fathers and grandfathers recall sleeping with dampened washcloths over nose and mouth to keep from breathing in the incessant dust that swirled around their homes, if they were lucky enough to keep them.

Edith Thomason's family had made the journey to California eight years before the Royals, abandoning its sharecropping section of the family farm in 1932 to live with relatives and work the California fields for more a year before returning.

"Oklahoma was literally blowing away, and I mean blowing away," Edith Thomason Royal said. "I can remember going to the fields to work or going into town for bingo and coming home during one of those storms.

"If you left dishes out on the counter or in the kitchen sink, they would be covered with sand. You could just see the shapes, the outlines of the dishes. You couldn't tell what anything was. I mean it was all red sand that had blown through the cracks and under the windows. It was awful."

The $10 the quickly maturing Darrell Royal paid the

Royal's parents, Katie Elizabeth and Burley, in 1910.

one-armed man for the ride home from California had been earned in the rich California groves over the past three months, picking fruit or vegetables, working on construction crews, loading trucks.

"Anything I could find," Royal remembers.

In late spring of 1940, Royal's father, Burley, had finally joined the parade of Midwesterners who headed west in search of greener pastures. Though he had steadfastly held on with one odd job or another and somehow kept his family off the government dole — Darrell and his three brothers often joined Burley in picking the stubby cotton that now was about all folks could squeeze out of the once-fertile Oklahoma soil — by the spring of that year Burley could see no other solution than to join the sad parade west down Route 66. With him, he took his second wife, and his two youngest sons, Darrell and Glenn, who was 4 years older.

Glenn and Darrell spent much of the summer sleeping in the trailer that Burley had built during the spring and pulled full of the family's furniture behind his once-new Whippet automobile. After Burley had sold his house, the Whippet was the sole remnant of a once-prosperous period when he earned a good living supplying farmers with petroleum products.

"We went to California because there was a chance of finding work out there," Royal said. "My stepmother's son had a place on a few acres out there and they had built a new house and they hadn't torn down the old one — so there was a place to live.

"My dad sold our place in Hollis and loaded up the furniture in the trailer he built. We had a Whippet, which my dad had bought new just before things got bad, when he had built a new house in town.

"I'm telling you. We could barely get over some of those mountains. Man, we must have had 20 flats on the way. The thing I remember most about that trip is how hot it was once we got to the desert and how many flats we had. We spent one night in a motel. We were all piled up in one room, but boy it was the nicest place I'd ever been in and certainly the nicest place I'd ever stayed.

"It probably wasn't much. But it impressed me at that age."

Royal never doubted his decision to go back to Oklahoma, though he might have begun to question the wisdom of his transportation when the one-armed man pulled out the first of a seemingly endless cache of pint whiskey bottles shortly after the journey began.

"I remember one day he got drunk when we were driving through the mountains, where the road rides right out on the edge," Royal said. "We had a blowout and we almost went over. I mean we stopped right at the edge and it was a long drop down. That wasn't the only time we almost went over. But I was too young to have sense enough to get out."

The odd couple parted one night in Abilene, Tex., close enough for Darrell to hitchhike up through Childress and home to Hollis, where he would live out his high school years with his Grandmother Harmon. The night before starting home from Abilene, he spent the night in jail after falling asleep on the Taylor County Courthouse lawn and being awakened by the night duty officer, who after hearing his plight offered him a softer bed and breakfast with the other prisoners.

Royal was glad to have both the bed and breakfast. And soon glad to be back in Hollis, not so much a kid anymore.

"I think my life changed because of age more than experience," Royal said. "I look back in retrospect and say that summer in California might have spurred me on, but at the time it didn't seem like a big push."

Indeed, Royal was easily able to slip back into the life of a rural, American town with a population between two and three thousand, depending on how many families were displaced at the time.

Though only out of junior high, Royal was already well known in his home town as an inquisitive, restless young man with an abundance of energy who was blessed with exceptional athletic ability and an already well-honed sense of competition.

"Anything competitive — baseball, basketball, football — Darrell was right in it," said Leon Manley, who grew up in Hollis a class behind. "That's what he was all about."

Manley played football with Royal for the Hollis Tigers and the Oklahoma Sooners and for him when Royal (at age 28) took his first head coaching job with the Edmonton Eskimos of the Western Interprovincial

Football Union — later the Canadian Football League.

Royal became an organizer early. He was constantly trying to round up enough players for a football game or a baseball game, or trying to talk his brother, Glenn, into running a foot race.

"He was always after me to run him a race," Glenn said. "I'd race him sometimes — and he was always pretty fast for his age — but I'd finally have to tell him go away. I didn't want to run anymore races."

Another one of Royal's favorite pastimes was handball, though not at the local spa, of which of course there was none.

"I remember buying one of those little red rubber balls for a nickel," Darrell said. "We'd go downtown to an old, abandoned

theater that only had three walls standing. We broke off some chalk from a piece of old sheet rock and drew some lines on the back wall and on the cement floor to line out the court."

No one to play with? No problem. Darrell had his own Olympic Games — against himself. With a rake, he graded level a sandy pit out back of Grandma Harmon's house that became a broad-jump pit.

"I'd put a stake out there and when I had no one to compete with, I'd just try and jump farther than that stake. I also had a wheel off an old wagon that I used as a discus. I didn't know anything about staying in a circle, but I'd stay behind a line I'd drawn in the dirt and try and throw that wheel as far as I could. When I hit the mark I was throwing at, I'd move it a little farther out.

"A lot of the games I played by myself, just competing against a better mark."

Royal also used to run sprints against cars that drove by his grandmother's house. He also ran his paper route on foot, all over town, and frequently ran most of the eight miles out to the Royal grandparents' house. Usually he would walk down the road until he was out of his grandmother's sight before breaking into a run, so she wouldn't get on him about heat stroke sure to strike down anyone who ran down the road under the summer sun.

The $5 that Royal earned sweeping out the Ford dealership — and later the money he earned from a more lucrative endeavor of shining shoes, he split with Grandma Harmon.

The two of them were especially close. Even when the Royals were living in their new house in 1929, the conditions were crowded. So frequently, young Darrell would excuse himself after supper and go to Grandma's house to sleep, to keep her company especially after Grandfather Harmon had died.

Royal never knew his mother,

STATE CHAMPIONS
MYTHICAL
Undefeated!

CONFERENCE CHAMPS
Southwestern + Twin Seven

GAMES		SCHEDULE		SCORES	THEY
			WE		0
			26		0
			39		0
			59	FORFEITED	
SEPT. 18	LONEWOLF				0
SEPT. 25	ERICK		13		14
OCT. 2	ELK CITY		25		0
OCT. 9	SAYRE		13		7
OCT. 16	HOBART		19		6
OCT. 23	CLASSEN		28		
NOV. 11	ALTUS				
NOV. 20	FREDERICK				
NOV. 26	MANGUM				

who died when he was 4 months old. When he was about 6, an older sister, Ruby, died of food poisoning. Another sister, Mahota — who had in some ways been a surrogate mother — also passed away several years later.

Darrell carried a sense of loneliness that was to follow him throughout his life, though he was always surrounded by a loving family, including his three protective, older brothers.

"Glenn tells me that I was spoiled when I was a little kid because I didn't have a mother," he said. "My aunts were always the mothers, and of course both my grandmothers."

So it was natural for Darrell to move in with Grandma Harmon when he returned from California.

"I remember we always went through a ritual when I'd come home late at night from being off playing a basketball game or a football game. Sometimes it was really cold, those nights would get pretty frisky; but I'd always knock on the front door and Grandma would say, 'Who is it?' And I'd say, 'It's me Grandma.' And she'd say, 'Oh, I'd know that voice in France. No one could fool me with that voice.'

"So then she'd start to unlock the door — which was locked with a nail driven into the left of the frame. And she'd twist the nail this way or that so the door would open. That was her protection."

Grandma Harmon always asked who won and more times than not, Darrell would reply, "We did, Grandma."

Then she would laugh and say, "Aw, you boys must have a terrible rep. I don't know why they play you."

On most of those cold nights, Darrell would slip into bed to find that Grandma Harmon had heated a flat-iron on the wood-burning stove in the kitchen, wrapped it in newspapers and slid it under the covers to the foot of her favorite grandson's bed.

A ruling by the local district committee that Royal was ineligible following his return from California — despite the fact he had lived in Hollis all his life and was sleeping in the same bed he'd slept in since the seventh grade — cost him his sophomore year of eligibility. But nevertheless, he never missed a day's workout and even

Royal and his three brothers, (clockwise from bottom left) Don, Ray and Glenn.

played in two football games. One was fairly safe — against a team of prisoners inside the fences of the Granite Federal Reformatory. He also played in the uniform of an injured teammate in a loss to a high school team in Oklahoma City, but he and Coach Wild decided that to engage in such shenanigans any further would endanger yet another year of eligibility.

Darrell did not play in any more games that season, but after practice he would spend extra time with one of his first loves, punting a football and studying the game he loved so well.

"I guess it was apparent since I was a kid which direction I was going, though I really didn't get any encouragement from anybody," Royal said. "Athletics was just something I excelled in, but I never looked at it as a way out."

He also immersed himself into a variety of business endeavors — another talent for which he remains astutely capable today.

For instance, Royal studied his shoe-shine competitors and soon learned the secret of a clean brush and shine rag. After football practice, he would go down and re-open Cecil Sumpter's barber shop and hustle shine business at 10 cents a pop with the crowd waiting for the

LaVista Theater to open for the night's business.

Royal also had a job feeding the printing press at The Hollis Daily News.

Oldest brother Ray, now in his 80's, recalled in 1976 that through his various enterprises, his younger brother actually got along quite well after coming back from California.

"Heck," Ray said, "he was making more money than most married men with families."

Joe Bailey Metcalf, who succeeded Wild as Hollis head coach before Royal's junior year, noted in an interview decades later, "Darrell was always wound pretty tight. He didn't have time for just sitting around. He worked about as much as any kid I ever knew. But don't think for a minute he didn't have time for other things. He was a leader in everything, including the mischief."

By the football season of 1941, America was still some months away from the shocking horror of the Japanese attack on the U.S. Pacific Fleet at Pearl Harbor. Quarterback Darrell Royal was the focal point of the coming season — as well as the object of some of his teammates' pursuit as fall practice began.

It was a tradition, Leon Manley recalled, that each player was to have a haircut as practice resumed. Seniors cut the juniors' hair and the juniors in turn butchered the sophomores' locks. Everyone pretty much accepted his fate — except Darrell.

"As I remember, Darrell used to wear striped overalls, and where the loop is for a hammer, he had a pair of scissors tied there," Manley said. "He cut everybody else's hair, but nobody could get to Darrell. They couldn't catch him. He was that fast."

What folks didn't know was that those striped overalls had once belonged to Ray. And they were not government-issue as many kids had to wear in those days. Royal kept them pinned tightly at the waist, so no one would know that he had no underwear.

The school grounds were out of bounds for hair cutting, but Manley recalls that frequently a gang of teammates would wait in hiding for Royal as he approached school in the mornings and would then try to ambush him during the noon recess as well.

"You'd see Darrell every day hoofing toward the school grounds with what looked like a dozen guys chasing him," Manley said. "I don't know that they ever caught him."

They didn't. But Royal got his hair cut, anyway.

"I finally got so embarrassed because I had cut so many people's hair and then dodged them all, that one day I finally just sat down and said, 'Get busy' and let them cut it," he said. "I was tired of being the only one in the crowd with hair, so I finally said they could just go ahead and cut it."

Dick Highfill became Hollis' new head coach before the 1941 season. He moved Royal to halfback and installed Clinton (Chief) Cunningham as the quarterback after two losses in what would eventually become a 3-8 season.

"I didn't know anything about calling signals," Cunningham remembered. "So after every play I would run by Darrell on the way to the huddle and he would tell me what play to call.

"As far back as I can remember, I guess Darrell was the best all-around athlete Hollis ever produced. You don't hear much about it, but he was a great basketball and baseball player. We won our district and qualified for the state tournament in baseball our senior season, but couldn't go because of the tire shortage."

The baseball season that Cunningham spoke about, right fielder-pitcher Darrell Royal struck out 38 of the last 40 batters he faced and was once offered a baseball scholarship at the University of Southern California.

But Royal was back at quarterback for his senior season in 1942, and the Tigers streaked to 10 consecutive victories — including a 27-14 victory over Oklahoma City power Classen High in which Royal threw two touchdowns and returned an interception 60 yards for another score.

Enid High also finished the season undefeated, and Coach Highfill challenged Enid to a game. Enid declined the opportunity, so Highfill and the Tigers declared themselves state champions.

"We had a pretty good football team," Royal said. "I think 13 of those guys eventually got scholarships that weren't academically related. We were pretty good for a high school football team."

But for the Hollis senior class of 1943, and for most young men of the era who had survived a childhood in which they were able to really be kids for so few years, college would have to wait. The world was at war.

Lank Smith
Left Halfback

Darrell Royal
Right Halfback

3RD AIR FORCE FOOTBALL TEAM
1945 SERVICE CHAMPIONS

CHAPTER THREE

Love and the Military

With His Country at War, Royal Meets His Future Bride and Volunteers to Serve

The summer of 1942 was immortalized by author Herman Raucher in his novel of the same name, a story of the last summer of innocence and the coming of age on Packett Island for three teenagers named Hermie, Oscy and Benjie.

"And they lay there on the dune over which the old house stood — Beau, John and Digby Geste, Devils of the Desert, steel in their hearts and sand in their Jockey shorts," Raucher wrote in this memorable classic.

That summer found Darrell Royal and his pals back in Hollis a few years older and perhaps more familiar with the feeling of sand in their Jockey shorts — those who had them.

The Japanese bombing of Pearl Harbor on December 7, 1941, had thrust America into a war that so many from an older generation who remembered the carnage and loss of World War I so desperately wanted to avoid. By the summer of the next year, the eligible young men of Hollis and countless other towns, large and small across America, streamed to hastily constructed receiving centers at new posts and bases that sprang up all across the country. The eldest Royal brothers joined the parade.

Don left early that year to join the war against the Germans in Northern Africa as an Army Air Corps P-38 pilot. He survived being shot down when pilots from his squadron strafed native tribesmen who often captured Americans and sold them to the Germans. Ray left and was eventually was put in charge of what developed into

a crack African American transportation unit that served in Europe. Glenn ended up in the Pacific in charge of an aircraft maintenance unit that kept the planes flying — the planes that helped turn the tide against the Japanese.

Among the 12 million men and women who were called in defense of world freedom, Royal's brothers never forgot the kid back home.

"They were good big brothers, everyone of them," Royal said with feeling. "When I was still in high school and they had gone in the service, they each sent me a little money every now and then. I've never forgotten that.

"It might be only $5 or whatever, but that was big; that was a week's pay at the Ford dealership. We always stayed in touch by writing. I've thought more of that since I've gotten older. I love them for what they did, more now than I did back then."

Royal recently was in Hollis. Among his stops was a visit to the modest granite monument on the lawn of the post office, where those who gave their lives in World War II are listed.

"I stopped and read all the names," Royal recalled. "It was a long list and of course I knew most of them. It gave me a funny feeling because there were a number of names there of boys that I played high school football with."

But during that summer before he would lead the Hollis Tigers to an undefeated season and a self-proclaimed state championship, love touched Royal in a way he had never felt for either his brothers or his teammates.

Edith Thomason was one in the many teenagers in and around Hollis who was fond of visiting the local skating rink, where roller-skating was only one of the popular pursuits. On this particular night, she was sleeping over with a girlfriend in town.

Royal was a star quarterback and halfback for the U.S. Army team in 1945.

"We had been skating, and Darrell's brother, Glenn (who had been dating Edith's friend, but would leave shortly on active duty) was going to walk the girl I was spending the night with home," Edith recalled. "Darrell happened to be with Glenn that night and so he walked along with us.

"It wasn't really a date, but that was the night I met Darrell and from then on for awhile, I would see him when I'd go to town. I thought he was pretty cute."

The feeling was apparently instantly mutual.

"I remember that night very well," Darrell said. "Yep, it was one of those love-at-first-sight deals, though it wasn't necessarily 'This is who I want to marry.' But I never even had puppy love. Edith is the only woman I have ever cared about."

Dating wasn't easy without transportation. And though Darrell got around easily afoot, it was not in those days fashionable for a young man to invite a young lady out for a jog. And Edith lived 20 miles outside of Hollis.

So in the early days of their courtship, they met casually on the summer streets of the small town; but not really by chance. Edith's sleepovers with her girlfriends in town became more frequent.

"I don't remember how we ever managed," Edith said. "I guess I just looked around for him and maybe he looked for me, because the town was pretty small and everybody went to town on Saturday.

"Everybody walked around if you didn't have a car. People who had a car would get to town early, so they could get a good parking place on the main street. They would all sit in or on those cars and watch the people go by. I don't think anybody does that anymore, but back then that's what we did. That's where we went to visit people."

Sometimes they would go to a movie together, or meet afterward when Darrell was through hustling shoe shines with the Saturday night crowd. Sometimes they would pile into someone's car until the seats overflowed and just ride around town, or park somewhere out in the country.

"Sometimes we parked and if you had a big group in the car, we'd all talk, tell jokes and laugh," Edith said. "We had a good time."

Sometimes the two young lovers would chance to sit together on a bench on the lawn around the courthouse, catching the breeze that would stir the shrubs and trees while they watched the Saturday night promenade. And it was on those occasions that Edith became aware of her beau's propensity for finding friendships in the strangest of places.

"There was a prisoner he knew, that he'd somehow struck up a friendship with and sometimes he'd talk to him while we were together," Edith said. "Darrell was always wandering around town alone in those days because he lived with his grandmother and he was lonely. He would just strike up friendships with almost anyone."

Royal once said he would rather be with someone he didn't especially like than to be alone.

"I don't like to be by myself," he admitted. "Where it comes from, I don't really know, but I like to be around people."

Royal well remembers — with some pathos — shouting back and forth to the residents of the local courthouse jail.

"Oh, yeah, we used to talk to those jailbirds. I used to get a big kick out of that; but I always felt sorry for them. I would talk to them and tell them what I would do to them if I could get to them. But they were enjoying it, too. They always asked if we were coming back."

Edith was not aware of Darrell's standing as the town's best young athlete when they first met that summer, though she would soon realize she had landed one of the town's prize young catches and its football hero.

"We lived out in the country about 20 miles and I went to a little school in Gould, which was about eight miles outside of Hollis on the highway," Edith said. "We were so small that we didn't have football; we had baseball and girls and boys basketball. So I didn't know anything about football. The first football game I ever saw was after I met Darrell and I decided to go see him play. That was the first time I ever even thought about football."

Even though Darrell was smitten, the two didn't exactly walk around town holding hands.

"In those days when we were kids in high school, when a guy went with a girl, he got teased. So a lot of the guys avoided girls because they would get teased," Leon Manley said. "Everyone teased Darrell about Edith. Every-

Edith Thomason at age 15.

Royal (second from right) and three Army buddies at Drew Field in Tampa, Fla. Often Royal and Lank Smith (right) were confused as twins.

one knew they were going together, but you seldom actually saw them together. And when people teased Darrell about Edith, he teased back."

Those idyllic days were numbered.

In the spring, Darrell Royal volunteered for the draft; but was stunned when he flunked the physical because of water on a knee. It was fashion in those days for young men of draft age to routinely be passed on their senior year. In the time between registering for the draft and taking his physical, Royal had stopped going to class. Now, he was forced to prevail on his teachers to help him catch up and graduate on time, because he knew his plans to someday attend college hinged in part on that diploma.

He passed a subsequent physical in July and would soon leave for basic training as a member of the Army

Air Corps, like two of his brothers.

By the summer of 1943, America was fully mobilized and was fueling the Allied war effort with money, petroleum, tanks, guns, ships, planes and ammunition as well as its young men and women. The tide had finally begun to turn in favor of the Allies.

In May, the Battle of North Africa ended, and Field Marshal Erwin Rommel fled to Germany. By mid-summer, the invasion of Italy had begun, and U.S. troops were retaking the Pacific from the Japanese while the Germans had finally been stalemated on the Western Front.

On the night before he was to catch an early morning bus to Fort Sill in Lawton, Darrell borrowed a car from his brother Ray's wife, Pearl, for a date with Edith, who wore a white dress with dark blue polka-dots. Parked under the stars of a still summer night, Darrell vowed that he would return from whatever fate held for him and the two of them would spend the rest of their lives together. Edith — who still had another year to finish in high school — promised to wait as had thousands of other young girls who pledged an undying, everlasting love to young men bound to become soldiers.

Though they did not know it at the time, a series of quirks, perhaps not unlike his surviving the auto accident some years later, would intercede in Royal's behalf over the next two years and prevent him from being shipped overseas.

But Royal was on the move. After a short processing period at Fort Sill, he was assigned to be trained as a tail-gunner and shipped to Miami for basic training. Somehow, the records of his training company were lost and all had to repeat the six-week basic training period. While there, Royal was once reprimanded by an officer during a field training break for enlisting a fellow trainee in a contest to see who could throw his dummy grenade the farthest.

But by now Royal had discovered an unsuspected benefit of being in the service — he like Army food. No, he loved it.

"I had been eating catch as catch can for a long time," he pointed out. "That was the first time I can ever remember having three meals a day that I could eat all I wanted.

"Boy I loved that gravy. I loved that breakfast, had all the milk I wanted. I even loved the food in basic training."

After Miami, a well-fed Royal was shipped to Harlingen, Tex., where he attended gunnery school and shot short-caliber guns. Though not especially fond of shooting machine guns, Royal did well enough to earn his silver aerial gunner's wings which he proudly wore home on furlough to visit Edith back in Oklahoma before again shipping out for tail-gunnery school at Davis-Monthan Air Base in Tucson, Arizona.

By the time Royal completed heavy bombardment training in Arizona in the spring of 1944, the Allies were secretly poised for their historic mass invasion on the beaches of Normandy in June. Fate again intervened in Royal's life. Of the 60 crews in his training squadron, 57 were shipped overseas. Three crews, including Royal's, were chosen for photo reconnaissance training at of all places, Will Rogers Field in Oklahoma City.

Finally, on June 26, 1944, almost exactly a year after

Darrell had left Hollis and a month after Edith had graduated from Gould High School, the two were married almost on the spur of a moment in Oklahoma City by a preacher at the First Methodist Church. Neither was old enough to vote. Darrell was 20, Edith not quite 19.

"They didn't have much money to live on, but neither did we," Edith's 93-year-old mother remembers. "I didn't know they would get so serious so quick, but we loved Darrell the first time we ever met him.

"I remember when they came home that night after they had gotten married, we were already in bed, but I was so glad to see them. Edith said, 'Mother, meet your new son-in-law.'"

The affection between Darrell and Edith's mother has been as lasting as the marriage.

"I told Darrell one time that I tell people he is the best son-in-law in the world," Mrs. Thomason said. "He told me I was the only mother he ever knew. I said if I had realized that, I would have tried to be a better mom. But I love him, and I think he loves me."

Darrell and Edith both call Mrs. Thomason "Mother," and Royal is well aware of her affection for him.

"I think the nickel's in the air over which would of us she would pick if we ever separated," he said with a laugh.

After a short honeymoon, Royal reported back to Will Rogers Field, where his crew was eventually reassigned for further training in weather recon again. The young married couple moved into a three-bedroom house with two other couples in Darrell's flight crew.

"We all had separate bedrooms, but we shared the living room and kitchen," Edith said.

They also shared expenses and all the wives worked to help supplement the meager incomes their husbands were getting.

"I tried being a waitress and got a job in the nicest hotel coffee shop in Oklahoma City," Edith said. "I lasted one week. I found out real quick that if I didn't flirt with those old men that I wasn't going to make any kind of tips. I was still a country girl and I'd never been around anything like that in my life."

Edith held other jobs, including selling discount photography coupons for Brown's Department Store. Among her samples were pictures taken of herself that showed off her striking good looks and long, attractive hair in the Veronica Lake style so popular during the 1940's.

On the Third Air Force team, Royal was a triple-threat back and a dangerous punt returner.

Three months after they were married, Edith discovered she was pregnant with their first child, Marian. And it was about that time that fate again reared its friendly head. Shortly before his crew was scheduled to be shipped out, Darrell experienced a sharp pain in his lower right abdomen.

He reported to sick call and was immediately rushed to the base hospital where an Army surgeon removed an acutely infected appendix. A new tailgunner was assigned to his crew and they shipped out.

But before his attack of appendicitis, Royal had become a star for a team called the Bombers in the base touch football league, gaining notice in a base newspaper that also took note of his operation:

"The Bombers received a severe jolt this week when 'Duke' Royal, their star passer and runner in all games thus far in the race, suffered a severe attack of appendicitis."

An officer later noticed Royal shooting baskets in the base gymnasium while he was mending from his operation and suggested he try out for the base basketball team.

Soon Sgt. Darrell, a.k.a. 'Duke,' Royal was the starting point guard for the Will Rogers Eagles and also played on a base baseball team while he awaited reassignment.

But by the spring of 1945, Allied victory was imminent. Adolph Hitler committed suicide, and Berlin fell early in May. Shortly thereafter, President Harry S. Truman announced the German surrender on May 8, 1945 — on what became known as V-E Day, victory in Europe. On August 6, the U.S. shocked the world by dropping the atomic bomb on Hiroshima and the days of the war in the Pacific were also numbered.

Royal was sent to Tampa, Fla., to try out for the Third Air Force football team. And it was there that another memorable character passed through his life — a German prisoner of war named Otto.

The two met working alongside one another on the

Drew Field baseball diamond, Royal as part of a duty detail and Otto as a member of a contingent of German prisoners being held there.

"It was strictly pick-and-shovel work," Royal said.

One day, the ever-curious young soldier struck up a "conversation" with the tall, blond and blue-eyed prisoner who worked alongside him. Otto's English was very limited, but Royal did learn that he had no idea what was happening to his family back in Germany.

"War is bad, but it's a tough situation when you meet a guy personally like that who has the same kind of family ties that you do. We could have very easily been trying to kill each other, but I couldn't help but click with him. It was obvious that we liked each other."

Football tryouts began shortly thereafter and Royal would see Otto infrequently during the next couple of months — though their paths would again cross — and he would sometimes stop by and give Otto and his fellow prisoners candy bars or some other such items — a move that was not popular with some of his fellow soldiers. This of course did not deter Royal, who relished being back in a football uniform.

One of the few players on the Third Air Force team who did not have college playing experience, Royal nevertheless moved into the single-wing backfield rotation as a substitute for all-Americans Charlie Trippi of Georgia and Bob Kennedy of Washington State. He also drew quick attention with his precision punting and punt returns, returning one for a 55-yard touchdown in the season-opening game in September.

Marian had been born in Tampa late in the summer, and the Royals moved from the home they shared with a former Hollis resident into a one-room apartment with a Murphy bed that folded down out of the wall, a sink in the corner and a bathroom down the hall they shared with other residents.

"It was tough living there," Edith said. "So before Darrell was to begin traveling with the Third Air Force football team, we decided it would be best if I went home to Oklahoma."

Royal moved into the barracks with other members of the team. It was there he made a lifelong friend in Lan-caster Smith, who had joined the service after a year at Notre Dame — where he would later return to star as a safety on the consecutive national championship teams of 1946-47. The two looked so much alike that that people thought they might be twins.

"Anyone who was around Darrell at the time — and I was quite a bit — got the impression that there was something special about this guy; that he was a cut above everyone else," said Smith, now retired in Dallas after a successful career as an attorney.

"Darrell was sort of an old head in a young body. There was a lot of depth to him. He was always two or three chess moves ahead of everybody else. I was always impressed with him, even at that age. And he was a heck of an athlete — a great basketball player, a good baseball player and a terrific football player."

It was while playing for the Third Air Force that college football coaches, who were scouring service teams looking for prospects soon to be discharged, noticed Royal and soon began to send him letters. Royal broke his wrist in the seventh game of the season, but stayed with the team through its final game of the season in December in Los Angeles.

After a short Christmas leave back home, Royal returned to Drew Field in Tampa, where he received a shock.

"Everybody was gone," Royal said. "I had no one to report to to find out what I was supposed to do to get discharged."

Ironically, he ran into Otto, whose English had improved over the past few months. It was Otto who got over to Royal that soldiers were being processed out across town at MacDill Field. Royal confirmed that and after spending the night on the base, boarded a bus for MacDill the next morning with his B-4 bag. As the bus approached the main gate at Drew Field, Royal and Otto saw each other for the last time.

Otto was mowing the grass near the gate.

"It was a strange deal," Royal remembered. "I saw him and stuck my head out the window of the bus so he could see me and I waved. He waved back. I felt sorry for Otto. I wish today I knew what happened to him and his family."

CHAPTER FOUR

A Sooner Star

Royal Punts and Passes His Way to Glory on the Oklahoma Gridiron

Lancaster Smith, who specialized in insurance law before he turned the reins of the Dallas firm he established over to his sons, on occasion used an anecdote to punctuate a message to a jury about to decide liability and damages.

"I used it sometimes when I wanted to illustrate a point that things don't always turn out the way you want them to, or wish them to, or think they will," Smith said.

Smith recalled a close friend in the service and how they were at a bull session one night when each member of the group would talk about his life's plan or alternatives that he might consider once mustered out of the armed forces.

His friend, Smith said, stated how he just might one day become a lawyer.

"When it was my turn, I said I wanted to be a football coach," Smith related to the jury. "Well, my friend, Darrell Royal, went on to become the great football coach at the University of Texas. And here I am as an attorney, trying this case before you here today."

Smith said the story never failed to produce at least one or two jurors who approached him after the case was decided and told him how much they enjoyed the story about him and Darrell Royal.

When the two friends mustered out of the service late in 1945, neither knew exactly what lay ahead. Smith, though he was mistaken about the profession on which he would eventually settle, knew he was going back to

Notre Dame — where he would finish law school in 1949 and even flirt with a little high school coaching while working as a young assistant in the Dallas district attorney's office.

Royal's future was less certain, though the longtime boyhood ambition of someday starring at the University of Oklahoma still burned in his heart.

"Oklahoma had always been my team," Royal said. "I remember when I was in junior high and a guy from Hollis who was playing at Oklahoma came back to visit his family. He wore that red leather jacket with the big white "O" around town and I just thought, 'Man, if I could only have one of those some day.' I followed him around so I could just look at that jacket."

When Royal's beloved Sooners played, he always tried to listen on the radio somewhere, often at the home of his friend, Don Fox.

"We used to put the radio out on his porch and play in the front yard and dodge the fire hydrant while we listened to the game," Royal said. "You'd hear that band playing on the radio and in my mind I was out there on that field, playing for Oklahoma."

When Royal was discharged from the service, he had a shoebox full of letters offering scholarships and other inducements, which at the time were not a major concern of the National Collegiate Athletic Association. Royal also had a $400 a week offer to play professionally in Canada, a princely sum but not an alternative that Royal seriously considered.

Oklahoma had offered the standard tuition, room and board and books. Royal nevertheless looked around to be sure he was making the right decision for himself and his young family. He made several visits two prospective

---

Royal, with professor C.F. Daily, was a popular student on the Oklahoma campus.

In 1949, Royal led Oklahoma to a national title and was honored as an all-America quarterback.

schools — and those schools wanting him would wire money, usually for round-trip bus fare. Royal, however, seldom traveled in such luxury.

"What he did was take that money and save it, then he would hitchhike back and forth to whatever school he was visiting," Edith said, laughing at the memory. "I found out about it one time when I was concerned that he should be home and I called the University of Tennessee, where he had gone to visit.

"They told me they had given him bus fare home, but somebody had seen someone that looked an awfully lot like him on the outskirts of town — hitchhiking. Darrell

UNIVERSITY OF OKLAHOMA FOOTBALL SQUAD 1948
BIG SEVEN CONFERENCE AND SUGAR BOWL CHAMPIONS

saved enough by doing that to buy us an old coupe that we ended up going to Oklahoma in."

Royal's hesitance to make a snap decision proved profitable in more ways than one.

Tired of traveling up and down the highway in the waning days of late winter, Royal decided it was time to commit to Oklahoma. He and Edith would somehow make do without any extra help, hoarding the money from his GI Bill — a stipend given to returning servicemen bound to go to college — and counting on his considerable enterprise, as usual.

That day, Royal walked from the one-room apartment he and Edith shared to the telephone office downtown to place a collect call to Norman and tell Sooner coach Jim Tatum that he would enroll for the spring semester.

"Normally, the route I took going in that direction downtown was on one side of the street. For some reason, and to this day I don't know why, I crossed the street and walked down the other side."

J.T. Cunningham's appliance store happened to be on that side. As Royal passed in front, Cunningham — an OU graduate — hollered at him from inside and said he'd been meaning to talk to him.

"When I got there, I told Mr. Cunningham he could call OU and tell them I was coming. I never did call them."

Once in Norman, Royal missed spring training — because of lingering problems with the broken bone in his wrist, suffered while playing for the Third Air Force. But he soon made an impression when practice began anew in the late summer, according to notice in The Norman Transcript.

"At Hollis several years ago, a skinny little newspaper carrier boy for The Hollis Daily News learned to peg his folded product so accurately from a moving bicycle (he sometimes borrowed from a brother) that he developed an uncanny accuracy at hitting porches.

"His name was Darrell Royal," the newspaper story told, "and pegging a football, he will try to hit that running throw for the University of Oklahoma this fall. In the Sooner summer camp drills, Royal ran promisingly from halfback off Oklahoma's new T-formation."

As a 159-pound freshman halfback, Royal was not an instant star. But he was a solid, productive player and became the Sooners' punter, place-kick holder and a top kick returner. And finally, he had enough footballs to kick. Royal frequently would outlast the equipment manager while he stayed after practice punting footballs —

As a punter, Royal was noted for his precision coffin-corner kicks.

either shagging them for himself or enlisting the help from the usually willing cadre of young schoolboys who daily tried to watch at least part of the Sooners' practice. In them, perhaps Royal found something reminiscent of a kid in hand-me-down overalls who used to haunt the sidelines of the Hollis Tigers' practice field.

The equipment man finally gave Royal a key to a stor-

age room so Royal could lock up the footballs and he could get home for supper. Before he went home, Royal frequently grabbed a quick plate of food that the kitchen personnel had saved him from the dining hall fare across the street from the practice field. Usually, dark was the only thing that stopped Royal's kicking.

"I don't remember ever having a football and not trying to kick it," Royal said. "A lot of kickers are not good punters because they never started out being a punter.

"As a little kid, I would go watch the high school workout and I'd get a ball and go kick it. I wanted to see if I could make it spiral. If I did anything well, that was it. I think I punted better than anything else I did."

Royal's punting at Oklahoma was to become legendary. But among his memories of that first season playing for the Sooners was his jarring introduction to the Texas-Oklahoma series, that at the time was being dominated by the Longhorns.

"The thing about the Texas-OU game — then and in all the ones I was involved in — was that both sides went on the field knowing they were going to get their fanny kicked," he said. "The only question was going to be who won.

"It always seemed to me that the contact was just stepped up a notch, you heard more racket. I don't know how it is now because I haven't been on the sidelines in more than 20 years, but that's the way it was then. You knew you were going to get beaten and bruised."

Royal's freshman season, Texas won its seventh, 20-13, in what would become a string of eight consecutive victories before Royal and his teammates would turn the tide in 1948.

But as things began to promise of a stellar future for Royal on the playing field, the lives of the young couple and others like them took on a little security, a little normalcy that many experienced for the first time. There was finally a time with no Depression, no Dust Bowl, no string of jobs that left little time for sleep, much less any form of relaxation, and no war.

"That's when my life really started to be fun," Royal said. "I hadn't had much fun going through that Depression. The

Royal rewards Bud Wilkinson after Oklahoma upset No. 3 North Carolina in the 1949 Sugar Bowl.

last years of high school were fun, but I knew that war was going on and that when I graduated I would be in it — because it didn't look like there would be any quick end to it.

"Even though I didn't get into combat, I was still in the military and you never knew when you would get out. So after that stage, as far back as I can remember, life wasn't that much fun. Starting in college is when I really began to have a good time. We had a fine bunch of

The Royal family in 1949: (Left to right) Edith, Marian, Mack and Darrell.

football players, most of who had come back from the service and you could see in time that we were going to have a good football team."

Merle Greathouse, an outstanding linebacker who had played one year previously, was one of those returning veterans to whom Royal became close. They remain good friends to this day. Royal and Greathouse, who settled in the oil business in Midland, Tex., were roommates on away games and on Friday nights when the Sooners would spend the night in Oklahoma City.

Their two young families lived two doors down across Flood Street from each other in Norman. Greathouse and Royal usually walked to class together.

"Darrell knew where he was going from day one," Greathouse said. "He was a great player, a great team leader and one of the most outstanding people I've ever had the privilege to know. He just has a knack for making people

feel at ease. He loves people and he loves his friends."

Even if sometimes, he did stretch his friends' attention span.

"None of us had much money, so we couldn't do much," Greathouse noted. "So we'd get a case of beer and go over to somebody's house and just shoot the breeze. The girls would talk about the kids, and all Darrell would talk about was football.

"Eventually we'd sit down with some paper and Darrell would take the offense and I'd take the defense. He'd draw offensive plays out of different formations and I'd try to come up with a defense to counter. He would do that forever."

Those notepad sessions with Greathouse were genesis to another strategy game Royal would later play with his quarterbacks, setting up defenses with the playing pieces on a checkerboard and challenging the quarterbacks to come up with plays that would work against a particular set.

Edith, too, fondly remembers those days and Oklahoma.

"There were about 25 married players on the team and quite a few kids. We'd all get together at somebody's house and just laugh and cut up. Our group was the strongest fraternity on campus."

The Sooners won seven of 10 games and won an eighth over North Carolina State in the Gator Bowl following Royal's wreck his freshman year. He played against State and later discovered that the lingering soreness he had felt since getting up from that farmer's bottomland pasture was gone.

Royal was injured off and on during his sophomore season. But he gave one of the more spectacular punting exhibitions of his career in a 21-12 upset victory over Missouri in 1947.

He punted out of bounds three times, including one kick that bounded out on the Tigers' three-yard line. OU recovered a fumble on the next play, leading to the touchdown that overcame a 12-7 Missouri lead.

By now, Royal was playing for new head coach Bud Wilkinson, who had been promoted from the existing staff when Tatum took the Maryland job. Greathouse tells this story about a game in Royal's senior year.

"Darrell punted out on about the 20, and Coach Wilkinson said to leave it where it was," Greathouse said. "But

Royal unleashes a booming punt against Tennessee in the 1950 Sugar Bowl.

Darrell comes in the huddle and says, 'Let's kick it over.'

"Now it was a rule of thumb that you didn't go against Bud's desires. But they voted in the huddle to go along, lined up again and he kicked it out on the five. If Darrell had been coaching that particular team, he would have ostracized himself and everybody else. Wilkinson chastised him pretty good, but he got away with it."

Years later, Royal would tell one of his star quarterbacks that if he ever waived off a play Royal sent in, he had better score with it.

As a junior, halfback Darrell Royal was a driving force in a 20-14 victory over Texas. He set up one touchdown with a run, hit two of three passes, kept the Longhorns boxed in with his punting and made three open-field tackles from his secondary position that most have agreed saved possible touchdowns. The Longhorns' run of eight consecutive victories — seven of them under UT coach D.X. Bible — came to an end. Texas' second-year coach, Blair Cherry, kept his players in

the locker room until the Cotton Bowl was empty.

"That was special," Royal said.

The Sooners, 9-1 in the regular season and undefeated in the Big Seven Conference, were headed to the Sugar Bowl that season against North Carolina. The Tar Heels featured a great triple-threat, all-American back with one of the greatest nicknames in college football history — Charley (Choo-Choo) Justice.

One Oklahoma newspaper wrote a story anticipating the matchup.

"Oklahoma has a busy little back of its own who will have the tough assignment in New Orleans of trying to match punts, passes and kick runbacks with the talented Justice."

The article noted Royal's durability, versatility and punting prowess, pointed out that a 38.5-yard punting average was deceiving "because he often kicks out of bounds to nullify enemy runbacks."

That season Royal had kicked out at the Texas A&M

one-yard line, the Iowa State two, Kansas State's six, 11 and 16-yard lines and boomed an 81-yard punt against Oklahoma A&M.

"The only time that Royal gets peeved," the article noted, "is when he gets his false tooth knocked out. That happens in virtually every game the Sooners play and also in many of the practice scrimmages. When it occurs in practice, all activity stops while everybody from OU coach Bud Wilkinson to the student manager tries to help Royal find his lost denture in the grass.

"I now carry that tooth in my pocket lots more than I do in my mouth," Royal laughed.

The newspaper story concluded by noting: "Justice still deserves his rating as the top triple-threat back in any bowl game this season. But Oklahoma believes that Royal, the frail little back with the disappearing false tooth, will do a good job at New Orleans."

A prophetic writer, indeed.

Royal averaged 45 yards on seven punts, rushed for 34 yards, threw a 43-yard pass to Frankie Anderson to set up one touchdown and threw a clearing block on George Thomas' touchdown run of 20 yards. On defense, he limited UNC's outstanding receiver, Art Weiner, to three receptions for only 28 yards. On Weiner's third catch, Royal hit him so hard he fumbled and Oklahoma recovered.

Fifth-ranked OU upset third-ranked Carolina, 14-6, for one of the biggest bowl victories in Big Seven history.

"It was an upset of a national level," said Royal, who caught the eye of at least one columnist covering the game, who pointed out that, "this Royal for Oklahoma was great. His punting was marvelous and his defensive play was really something to see, folks."

The Daily Oklahoman on the following day had a front-page picture of Royal kissing Wilkinson on the cheek — opposite a shot of a dejected Justice slumped on the bench with a towel over his head. The Oklahoma Senate passed a congratulatory resolution.

That was far from the only time Royal would receive accolades for his defensive ability. He still holds the OU career interception record of 17.

"Yeah," Royal said, "I dogged a few. But I think I

learned the footwork and a lot about how to play pass defense playing military football.

"There was a guy on the team who was past the point of being any good because he had been out of shape for too long. His name was Bob Andridge and he had played at Tennessee. He took interest in me and he found a willing pupil. He would get out to practice early and work on the footwork with me — how to change directions with the receiver — and I did that all the way through college.

"We played zone most of the time, except in that Sugar Bowl when I was assigned to cover Weiner man-to-man."

The Sooners approached the 1949 season with much anticipation and Royal was hailed as proper heir to quarterback Jack Mitchell. No less than immortal sportswriter Grantland Rice jumped on the Sooner bandwagon in his annual fall football forecast for *Look* magazine.

"For the past six years," Rice wrote, "it has been easy to name college football's national champion in September. It would be Michigan or Notre Dame or Army. This year, it is different. At least some dozen and a half teams have a possible shot at (the) number-one ranking.

"It is impossible to assay them against one another and declare that any two or three stand out. But if I were surrounded by king cobras and forced to make a selection, I would nominate Bud Wilkinson's big, fast, deep, aggressive University of Oklahoma squad.

"The Sooners have Darrell Royal to replace Jack Mitchell at quarterback. Others headed for all-conference honors are backs Lindell Mitchell and George Thomas, end Jim Owens, tackle Wade Walker and guards Norman McNabb and Stan West."

OU was indeed tough that season in compiling an 11-0 record, including a 35-0 victory over Louisiana State in its consecutive Sugar Bowl and its 15th consecutive victory. The Sooners, however, would finish the season ranked No. 2 behind Notre Dame in some polls and No. 1 in one.

And Royal again played a vital part in another victory over Texas, by the score, 20-14.

In his lead story for The Fort Worth Star-Telegram, Gene Gregston wrote:

"If University of Oklahoma coaches had any moist-palm fears when Jack Mitchell departed the Norman campus, they apparently did not tell Darrell Royal about them. For this man of many talents handled things here Saturday on the Cotton Bowl's lush, green turf as if he were the first and best-ever to take the ball from center.

"He punted (once for 71 yards), he passed (once for a touchdown), he ran (12 times for 34 yards), he was a bundle of alertness on defense; but more important, he led the Sooners with fine play selections on those devastating land drives to touchdowns.

"And during it all, the 170-pound, 3-year veteran was taking a brutal physical beating that forced him out of the game — but not for long."

Royal was chosen the all-American quarterback for 1949 and emerged from college wise about Wilkinson's cutting-edge, Split-T offense and confident of his place in the world.

"There were people during the Depression — doctors, the hardware store owner, the guy who owned a drug store and soda fountain — who weren't making much money; but they sure were making more money than people who didn't have jobs," Royal said.

"As a kid growing up, I never felt like I belonged with that crowd, so I grew up with quite a complex. Athletics got me out of that. Because I was a starter and a player on some outstanding football teams at Oklahoma, I lost a lot of that complex."

As a telling footnote to his college playing days, as a senior Royal was selected one of the Outstanding Sooner Men — by the college of business administration.

During graduation practice at Oklahoma, young Mack Royal attempts to join his dad on stage.

A Coaching Road Begins

An Eight-Year Journey, With Eight Coaching Stops, Leads to a Dream Job in Austin

For more than 15 years, Chris Schenkel was the voice of college football on the ABC television network. He is also remembered as the guy who made TV bowling actually interesting.

But as college football's top announcer when the game of the week was the ABC-TV Game of the Week (1964-81), Schenkel met — and frequently made friends with — many of the coaching greats of the post-World War II generation.

He counts Bear Bryant, Bud Wilkinson and Darrell Royal as his top three coaches. And though he hesitates to put them in any numerical order, he admits some prejudice toward Royal — who shares his affinity for Native American and western art, among other common interests.

Royal, with two key Mississippi State players, led the Bulldogs to a pair of 6-4 seasons.

"Darrell is right in there among my top three of all time," Schenkel said. "And I don't know where to place him — whether number one or number two, though I don't think number three. But he, of course, learned so much more than anyone else could have from my friend, my colleague and partner — Bud Wilkinson."

Royal soaked up every ounce of knowledge he could from the man who is as much the legend in Oklahoma as Royal is in Texas and was his head coach his last three years in a Sooner uniform.

"Bud liked Darrell's intensity and his competitive nature," remembered Schenkel, who spent many hours with Wilkinson and worked for 12 consecutive seasons in the broadcast booth with him as his color analyst. "He always said that Darrell was unbelievably focused. They were a wonderful combination. I've never seen such mutual respect between professor and pupil."

They formed a bond from the beginning. Wilkinson was the backfield coach at Oklahoma before he ascended to the head coaching job when Jim Tatum departed for Maryland, where he was to make his coaching name. And as much as Royal felt an obligation toward his coaching mentor, so too did the professor realize a debt to perhaps his most famous pupil.

Writing in a 1969 article in The Dallas Morning News, Wilkinson explained:

"I have always felt a special debt of gratitude to that first Oklahoma team and to Darrell. He played a very significant role in giving me the opportunity to have a career in coaching. The career, I've always believed, hinged to a great degree on the Missouri game of 1947.

"Oklahoma under Jim Tatum had a great year in 1946 and it was assumed by our fans that we'd have another.

CHAPTER FIVE

Royal served as an assistant on Beattie Feathers' staff at North Carolina State in 1950.

Overlooked generally was the fact that we had lost some excellent players to professional football.

"There was also the inevitable criticism to the effect that I was too young and too inexperienced to be a head coach. This increased considerably as we won only two of our first five games. When we faced Missouri, favored to win the conference, my future was in doubt.

"That's when Darrell helped make me acceptable as a coach to our fans. He was one of the most intelligent, dedicated players I've ever known."

Wilkinson then cited Royal's strategic punting exploits against the heavily favored Tigers and how it played a game-turning role in the eventual 21-12 victory that provided the impetus for the season-ending push to a 7-2-1 record.

"It is no surprise that Darrell has become a great coach," Wilkinson continued in the 1969 article, written a week after the Longhorns' historic victory over Arkansas in the "Big Shootout."

"He has the organizational ability, all the qualities of leadership and the soundest possible tactical understanding of the game. Equally important, he has the ability to earn the loyal support of the many and diverse factions involved

TEXAS COLLEGE FOOTBALL LEGEND **DARRELL ROYAL**

in a college program — rabid alumni, faculty members, student body, press, players' parents and girls, coaches' wives and so on. This support is essential if the football program is to be successful and a credit to the institution."

Royal did not desert the Oklahoma practice field when he finished his eligibility. He continued to sit in on coaches' meetings and quiz Wilkinson on aspects of the Split-T offense, which would become his offensive scheme during the early years of his own head coaching career.

Royal was so well schooled in the offense and Wilkinson so trusted him that he frequently appointed Royal to explain the intricacies of the system to visiting coaches who came to spring training in 1950. Among the coaches Royal spent time with was Kentucky coach Bear Bryant — with whom he would later develop a close, lasting relationship — and Beattie Feathers, the head coach at North Carolina State, a contact that would pay off shortly thereafter.

But the young Royal learned not only X's and O's from Wilkinson, he picked up some of his gentle manner — though Royal was never quite the mellow coach that Wilkinson was.

"I think at times I was more caustic and blunt than he was," Royal admitted. "But I learned from him that you get more from praise than you do from jumping on people.

"I learned that pride is the best possession you have. When you take the pride away from a player, you've destroyed the best tool you've got. If you've hurt him, you've hurt the team. So if you've got something that would really put him down, don't do it in front of the team. Do it in the office."

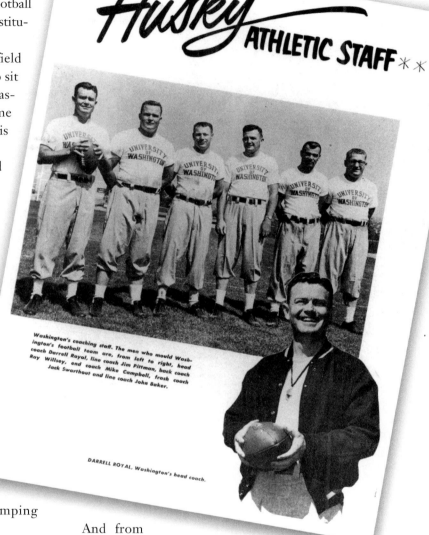

Washington's coaching staff. The men who mould Washington's football team are, from left to right, head coach Darrell Royal, line coach Jim Pittman, back coach Roy Willsey, and coach Mike Campbell, frosh coach Jack Swarthout and line coach John Baker.

DARRELL ROYAL, Washington's head coach.

Royal, with his two sons, Mack (left) and David, at the University of Washington in 1956.

And from Wilkinson, Royal also gleaned his basically conservative offensive philosophy — one that despite the many celebrated gambles he took over his illustrious career would one day earn him the tag as the Barry Goldwater of college football.

"I coached the same philosophy that Coach Wilkinson taught me," Royal said. "That it's a game of first downs — get the first down and then go to work on the next one, and another, and another and then you've got a touchdown. Don't try to get it all at once.

"That type philosophy requires a good short-yardage

Royal and his family enjoy a warm holiday fire prior to his departure to Austin in December 1956.

offense. And I think to be a great offensive football team, you've got to be able to make short yardage. To me, it's more important than overcoming third-and-long.

"You can always punt and play defense and then get a chance to start over again with first down. But there always comes a time in a game — always — when short yardage comes up. If not out in the middle of the field, it damn sure comes up on the goal line. And if you are not a good short-yardage team in the middle of the field, you can forget having a good goal-line attack."

The run-and-shoot offense of the late 1980's certainly reinforced that belief.

"It still comes down to getting used to knocking it out and grinding it out that makes you a better football team on the goal line," Royal continued. "Two areas of (offensive) football are really important — taking it out from your own end and taking it in.

"Don't make a mistake taking it out. And when you get down there, make sure you have enough muscle to take it on in. That stuff in the middle of the field is for entertainment anyway. That's old-timey thinking; it isn't the modern football, I know. But that was my philosophy."

Royal had actually taken a job as a head football coach at El Reno (Oklahoma) High School at mid-term, where he briefly taught two classes during the spring of 1950 and drove back and forth to Oklahoma's spring practices. To have just such a job was once Royal's only ambition, though he would actually draw only two paychecks and never stand on the sidelines during a game as a high school coach.

"When I got up toward high school graduation, I thought if I could make it as a college player, get out and get me a job as a high school coach in somewhere like Hollis, I would be happy," Royal said. "So talk about lofty ambition, then I didn't really have any.

"But then after meeting a few people in college and that spring afterward, I started thinking about greener pastures. I had loftier ambitions."

Royal interviewed that spring for an assistant's job at Vanderbilt — where they ran the straight-T of which Royal was less familiar; but that was the only time in his career that he was turned down for a position.

"I tried never to put myself in that kind of a situation again," he said.

He actually turned down an offer to interview for the vacant head coaching position at Abilene Christian College because he wisely felt he wasn't ready. But he jumped at the offer in March from Feathers to join his staff and help install the Split-T at North Carolina State. He also persuaded Feathers to hire former Sooner teammate Wade Walker to work with the offensive line.

Accolades came quickly for Royal. Former OU coach Jim Tatum paid him special credit after State upset his No. 8-ranked team at Maryland, 16-13. Royal — who scouted Maryland — noticed the Terrapins' quarterback tipped off his plans before he made a pitchout to the trailing halfback. So Royal suggested, and Feathers went along, that their defensive ends often should crash in on the quarterback before he had time to get into his rhythm. The strategy proved pivotal, and Tatum was highly complimentary in his post-game remarks.

After the season, Royal delivered an impressive lecture on the Split-T at a Tennessee coaching school and soon after was offered a job as backfield coach at Tulsa. He took it, not knowing that Wilkinson was also trying

Another Fine Picture From *Laughead* PHOTOGRAPHERS

In 1952, Royal spent a season on Murray Warmath's staff at Mississippi State.

to contact him about a recent vacancy at Oklahoma. He found out by accident, when he stopped to spend the night with a friend in Oklahoma City.

Royal talked to Wilkinson, told him he had just accepted a job at Tulsa, but would see if coach Buddy Brothers would let him out of his commitment. Brothers told Royal he thought a deal was a deal and Royal

had to agree. What might have happened if Royal had joined Wilkinson is but conjecture, another matter of providence.

Unknowingly, Brothers had appealed to Royal's strong sense of honesty, of sticking to one's word, that he inherited from his father.

Burley Royal never paid much attention to his

youngest son's athletic endeavors. He was still in California trying to make an honest living when Darrell emerged as a star in his last two years in high school. Darrell guesses that his dad saw him play twice at Oklahoma and witnessed only two games during his long coaching tenure at Texas.

"He never really talked to me a lot," Darrell said, "so it sounds like he didn't do anything for me.

"But one time I bought something at the five-and-dime variety store and they gave me too much change in pennies. It couldn't have been much, because I didn't have more than a dime. But when I discovered it, I went back and gave them back their money. Now when my dad found out about that, it really pleased him.

"Whatever I did, coaching or anything else, he didn't seem to care. He gave me more attention for giving that money back than anything else. So I would say that there is only one guy that I owe a cent to — it's $5 — and that's to a guy in the service. We got separated and I never got to pay him back. I would gladly give him $5,000 now just to get if off my conscience.

"I pay my debts and I stick by my word, because my dad was a real stickler for that. And I would rather have that than have had him bragging on me over what I did athletically and not give a damn about the other stuff."

As it turned out, Royal profited greatly by staying with his commitment to Tulsa. Brothers gave Royal a free hand with the offense, including instructing his quarterbacks from the press box during games. And after the 1951 season, Royal moved again. This time it was to join Murray Warmath's staff at Mississippi State, yet another move that would eventually prove providential.

That was Royal's last job as an assistant coach. At the suggestion of a former teammate who was playing in Canada, the Edmonton Eskimos decided to take a chance and interview this young American who had never been a head coach.

Knowing next to nothing about Canada or Canadian football, Royal nevertheless jumped at the chance to run his own show. It was, he said in retrospect, one of the best decisions he ever made.

"I always trusted that gut feeling," Royal said. "You ask why did I take this job? Why did I jump off and go to Canada and coach a professional team one year? It just seemed like a good thing to do.

"I got a chance to be on my own at a young age (28), to be a head coach. I didn't realize then how much that experience would help me later."

As happened in all but that one interview for the job at Vanderbilt, Royal was an instant hit with the Edmonton hierarchy, who chose him to succeed Frank Filchock — who after leading the team to the Grey Cup series for the first time in 30 years jumped to Saskatchewan after a contract dispute.

A local columnist observed at Royal's hiring, "He was only in Edmonton a few days to confer with Eskimo grid officials, but he left a wonderful impression."

The same columnist also called the young coach, "a handsome collar ad ... a country boy with Park Avenue talents and instincts."

One with a lot of work to do, especially when he announced he planned to use the Split-T, truly a foreign offense to Canadian professional football. Royal also faced a problem of dealing with players older than he. But with Claude Arnold, the former OU player who recommended him for the interview, and a few other former Oklahoma players he imported such as halfback Billy Vessels, Royal had some players on his side.

One of those pivotal in helping Royal establish himself — especially when he announced at the first team meeting that beer would no longer be iced down in the Eskimos dressing room — was his old high school and college teammate, Leon Manley.

Manley had played two years with the Green Bay Packers, but shoulder and knee problems convinced him he should turn his efforts to coaching. He decided, however, to join Royal when his old friend offered him more money to play in Canada than he had made in the National Football League.

Perhaps Manley was unaware that in addition to his blocking and tackling ability, Royal wanted him for another purpose.

Royal had one player, a lineman, who was leading a small band that resented taking orders from this kid from the States who had never even been a high school head coach in battle. And Royal had been catching a little heat from that faction for bringing in all his old Oklahoma buddies.

"Leon was a big, strong, muscular guy," Royal said. "When we were in college, before those spring scrimmages, all those linemen would run to the list of teams that were posted in the locker room to see who had to line up in front of Leon.

"For some reason, he never made all-conference or all-American, but he was one hell of a player. A bulldog. A real fighter. So the first day Leon comes in, I set up a scrimmage and I lined Leon up against the player who had been giving me a hard time. Leon worked him all over the field."

Afterward, Royal had no more disciplinary problems and both players became important contributors to the team. And his Split-T offense became the rage of the Western Interprovincial Football League in 1953, leading the league in total offense as the Eskimos won 12 of 16 games, before losing the best two-of-three Grey Cup series to Winnipeg.

"I learned more in that one year than in any other year of coaching," Royal said.

"That was my first year of dealing with the press. I learned to deal with a board of directors, which is kind of like the administration in college. I had weekly meetings with them. My alumni was the city of Edmonton. I had a weekly luncheon where I showed film and rehashed the game — showing them how we did well and why we failed. They had never had anyone do that in that kind of detail.

"So it was a good experience. Perfect training for me to come back and go into college football."

In 1954, Warmath was leaving Mississippi State, whose administration offered a four-year contract at $15,000 a year to lure Royal back from Canada. Though the Edmonton directors originally balked, Royal talked them out of holding him to the remaining two years on his contract, with everyone departing as friends.

Club president Ken Montgomery said, "We hate to see him go, but we felt like he deserved his chance."

Royal had not planned to bail out after only one year in Canada. But again, he went with what his intuition told him.

"That was another of those gut feelings, a common sense thing that said I'd better get out of there. For one thing, I got almost double my salary and I knew I had a job.

"I got up there and looked around and saw there were only nine jobs up there and that if you failed, there was no place to land. And I knew if I stayed up there too long, I would lose my contacts in the States. And I had grown a little. I thought I was ready to come back."

Royal's two teams at Mississippi State each posted 6-4 records. But two more years in Starkville, Mississippi, were enough for both Darrell and Edith — who left with mixed feelings.

"I loved Starkville," Edith said, "but I probably would have been run out of town on a rail if we stayed there much longer, because I found out I was pretty much — well — a liberal. Let's just say I would have had the Civil Rights legislation passed a long time before it was.

"I thought I had lived in the South when I moved there and that really proved interesting. My neighbor on one side was from Minnesota. On the other side was a Starkville native. They told me later that they had met at the clothesline one day and the girl from Minnesota asked the Starkville native if she had met her new neighbor. The girl from Mississippi said, 'No, but I heard her talking, and I know she is a damn Yankee!' "

Edith said it did not sit well with some of her acquaintances that she paid her housekeeper more than other people did and that she bought clothes for the housekeeper's children — including a newborn son

whom the woman named Darrell Royal Reese.

Royal also knew his future did not lay at Mississippi State, though he turned down an offer after his first year from a retiring Don Farout to succeed him at Missouri — which eventually hired another promising young coach named Frank Broyles.

"I told Coach Farout that I appreciated him thinking of me, but that I had signed a long contract and had already bounced around so that I thought I should stay," he said. "So I stayed another year and we worked our butts off, and then Ole Miss comes in and nabs the best players at the end of recruitment."

So when the University of Washington called after the next season, Royal drove to Memphis to meet with the Huskies' new athletic director, George Briggs, who was trying to salvage a program racked by a scandal involving illegal payments to players and recently slapped with a two-year probation by the Pacific Coast Conference.

"I took the job at the University of Washington without ever visiting the campus. I didn't need to," Royal said.

"It was obvious to me that Mississippi State was a place where it was going to be very hard to win. I looked at Washington's record over Washington State through the years. I looked at their attendance and the size of their stadium. I looked at their football budget. And I took the job."

He did not find a warm reception. His $17,000 salary raised cries of protest in the student newspaper, which polled the faculty and found 80 percent thought the salary too high and almost that many who thought football should be de-emphasized.

After the season began, however, a local columnist wrote, "Almost unnoticed is how well Coach Royal has handled what might have been a grave problem ... No favorites, no discrimination, a fair deal for all. And Coach Royal has complete harmony in the ranks."

Harmony in Seattle didn't last long after the Huskies completed a 5-5 season by upsetting Stanford and defeating Washington State, 40-26, in the traditional season-ending game.

The youngest coach in the Pacific Coast Conference was soon to be on the move again — and for the last time.

CHAPTER SIX

Leader of the Longhorns

A New Coat of Paint and a New Attitude Are Royal's Building Blocks

After the 1954 season, Mississippi State head coach Darrell Royal had been invited to speak at the annual coaching school of the Texas High School Coaches Association, which was being held that year in San Antonio.

While heading back to Starkville, the Royals passed through Austin. Darrell turned off the highway and took a detour through the campus of the University of Texas, which included a slow, round-the-block drive around the stadium that 40 years later would bear his name.

"I don't know, I just got a funny feeling that we would be back there someday," Royal remembered. "It was real spooky."

Based on experience with similar spooky feelings, the Royals should have put a down payment on a house while they were there — though that might yet have been a little premature. Destiny was not quite ready to make the call.

Texas coach Ed Price then was approaching what would be the final two years of his tenure.

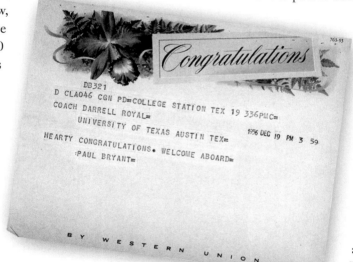

The Royal family upon their arrival in Austin in 1957.

A former three-sport letterman at the university, Price succeeded Blair Cherry, who was successful in his four seasons as head coach but only beat Oklahoma once in four tries — thanks in part to Royal himself. Price's 1952 team won an undisputed Southwest Conference title, established new school offensive records, defeated Tennessee, 16-0, in the Cotton Bowl and was ranked 10th nationally.

Under Price in 1953, Texas shared the title with Rice — an SWC power during the decade along with TCU — and finished 7-3 with a No. 11 ranking. But the Longhorns slid to 4-5-1 the season before Royal passed through that summer on his way back to Mississippi. They would manage to break even at 5-5 in 1955 before plummeting to 1-9 and a cellar finish in the SWC for only the second time in a long and proud history. That ignoble finish led to Price's dismissal by athletic director Dana X. Bible — who himself had been called to resurrect a failing football program in 1937 and ended a lustrous coaching career with a decade at Texas after leaving his mark both at Nebraska and Texas A&M.

Bible succeeded in bringing Texas back and won three SWC titles in 10 seasons. He and his successors left many

Royal and his first coaching staff at Texas in 1957. The Longhorns posted a 6-4-1 record.

Texas followers, however, yearning for more and wondering if the Longhorns could ever achieve the kind of sustained national recognition that Oklahoma was now enjoying under Bud Wilkinson.

"Darrell Royal accomplished things at Texas that a lot of people really never thought would be accomplished here," Rooster Andrews said. "And let me explain that a little. Everyone thought that Mr. Bible was going to bring us to the pinnacle ... they really did. And when that did not happen, then I think a lot of people thought well, if Mr. Bible can't do it then it can't be done here at the University of Texas."

Price's sliding record was only the symptom of deeper ills.

T. Jones, an all-SWC quarterback and SWC total offense leader for the Longhorns in 1952 under Price, had joined his former coach's staff prior to the 1956 season after serving two years in the Army. He did not step into a cohesive situation.

"It was an eye-opener," Jones said. "We really had a split staff. We'd come out of staff meetings and we'd get out onto the practice field and I'd see things — kids doing things certain ways — that were not the way they had

been talked about in the meetings. And I think there were certain coaches on the staff who would have liked to have had Ed Price's job. It was just a very unpleasant year for a rookie coach like myself."

Legend has it that when Bible let Price go after a 34-21 loss to fifth-ranked Texas A&M, he had a list of more than 100 prospective candidates. Some would be considered for the dual post of coach and athletic director, since Bible planned to retire, and some would be considered only as coach.

"I know I wasn't on any list. But for some reason I kind of felt like I might have a chance," said Royal. "I just felt like the cherry was ripe for pickin'."

Royal long had coveted the job and thought it would be a better place to make his career coaching stand than at his alma mater, a feeling that would later manifest when Wilkinson retired and again when successor Gomer Jones was fired in the mid-1960's.

Looking back with 20-year hindsight, Royal admits he still ponders the question: Why me?

"I've thought about that a lot," he said.

"I have said this many times and people think I am being modest and I'm not — there are a lot of people who never got the chances I got, who could have done equal to what I did. And I know that. I know that within my own heart.

"Why did I get this opportunity? I know a lot of good coaches who have been hurt and scarred when things didn't work out for them. They had miserable seasons and got fired. Coaches who if they had had the same opportunity I had could have had happen to them, what happened to me."

Of course there is the possibility that Royal just made more of the opportunities he had.

"Well, I don't think I screwed it up," he said. "But there were a lot of guys who had the same ability who were never in the right place at the right time."

Still, Royal had that knack — that gut feeling — of knowing when and where to be. Knowing when to hold 'em and when to fold 'em.

"There were some coaching jobs that I had that I don't think I could have stayed in for 40 years. Without getting into them specifically, all you have to do is look back at them and see. But I appreciate every job I had and the opportunities they gave me — to grow and learn in my chosen profession.

"Mr. Bible was at Texas for a long time. Texas is the type place you can go and stay. The elements are all there, the things that give you a chance to win. I think about it every time I say, 'It happened to me.' But there are a bunch of guys out there who could have done the same job if they'd been in the right spot."

The question is, how could anyone not have perceived — as Royal did — that Texas was the kind of place where you could have a pretty good shot at getting your name on something other than a bathroom wall?

No one will ever know how many rejections Bible received in his search. Nor why some of those contacted did not see the infinite possibilities that a 32-year-old Darrell Royal did. But history does divulge that Georgia Tech's Bobby Dodd and Michigan State's Duffy Daugherty — two of the era's most prominent coaches — were at the top of Bible's list.

As frequently happens in such situations, after prominent coaches turn down offers to discuss another job, they are contacted again for recommenda-tions. Just such a sequence of events thrust Royal into the Texas picture.

"The way I understand it, I was not on the list until the chairman of the Board of Regents (then Tom Sealy), called both Coach Dodd and Coach Daugherty and they each separately recommended me," Royal said.

The name, of course, was not unfamiliar to the Regents, the members of the search committee or to Bible.

Royal directs traffic during spring practice in 1957.

All remembered well the hand that Royal had played in ending Texas' eight-game string of victories against the Sooners in the late 1940's. By 1956, Oklahoma had won eight of the last nine games against the Longhorns and the last five in a row — including a 45-0 thrashing in the previous season. Royal was the guy who helped start all this losing mess to Oklahoma.

Interestingly, Royal had a preliminary inquiry from SMU athletic director Matty Bell, who had just fired Chalmer Woodard and would eventually hire Bill Meek. Royal didn't tell Bell he was not interested, because he had already realized he eventually wanted to get back to the Southwest. But he was keeping close contact on the behind-the-scenes dealing at Texas through an old friend, Tonto Coleman. It was Coleman, on Dodd' staff at Georgia Tech at the time, who had invited Royal in 1950 to interview for the job at Abilene Christian. Coleman told Royal that he had been recommended to Texas by both Dodd and Daugherty, but could offer little encouragement.

On a Saturday night in early December, however, as Edith and Darrell had just settled in for the night, the phone rang. When Royal answered, he heard on the other end the deep, booming baritone voice of Dana X. Bible. Royal momentarily put his hand over the phone and said, "Edith, this is it. It's the University of Texas."

Early the next day, Royal was on a plane to the Lone Star State after telling the Washington athletic director where he was going and that he would probably take the job if offered. He spent the night at The Adolphus Hotel in Dallas registered under the name of Jim Pittman, one of his assistants, and flew to Austin where he was picked up at the airport by Bible.

"I remember the airport still had barbed-wire around it," Royal said. "Mr. Bible picked me up and things happened awfully quick. He took me to see the president. I met with the athletic council, and then they took me to meet with the board of regents. In four hours, they had offered me the job."

Royal visits with Heisman winner Tom Harmon in the press box at the 1958 Cotton Bowl.

Royal accepted, phoned home with the good news, and Edith and the families of his coaching staff started packing. When the news broke the next morning, there was surprise in Austin and anger in some quarters on the West Coast.

Columnist Will Connolly of The San Francisco Chronicle had the opinion that Royal's leaving was "a slap in the face" to the University of Washington and wrote that Royal was "an inferior person who doesn't remain in one place long enough to vote."

But Washington AD George Briggs said, "I regret this loss very much. I feel (Royal) is one of the outstanding young coaches in America. He has my very best wishes for success at Texas."

All-Pacific Coast Conference guard Dick Say expressed the feelings of the team.

"We couldn't have been more surprised if someone had dropped a bomb. He had the whole school behind him. The spirit of the entire school came up more this year than any of the years since I've been here. He certainly accomplished a lot in a short time."

Say's surprise was equaled around The 40 Acres, as so well captured in Lou Maysel's lead in the Tuesday afternoon edition of The Austin American-Statesman:

"The University of Texas, which had announced it was seeking a veteran name coach, pulled a shocker Tuesday."

Bible said, "Royal is one of the comers in the profession. The University was fortunate to attract such a promising young coach."

Sealy, not naming his sources at the time, said, "Two of the nation's foremost coaches advised us that Royal is one of the most brilliant coaches in the collegiate football ranks."

And at his introductory press conference, Royal offered early indication of his exceptional quoteability.

"The first inkling that I had that I was in line for the Texas job came during a luncheon break while a committee of the board was interviewing me," he said.

"We had taken time out for a sandwich and a glass of milk and the talk got around to duck hunting. I told about our home in Washington being right on Lake Washington and how our kids used to feed the wild ducks when they came up into our yard. I told them about the day we came home from town and found that someone had left the back door open and the wild ducks had walked right up into the house.

"One of the regents looked at me and said, 'Anyone who can tell a story like that is going to make a great Texan.'"

After being offered the Longhorn's job, Royal returned to Seattle to gather Edith, Marian (11), Mack (9) and David (4). Despite leaving Edith's suitcase sitting in the living room, Royal sped out of their Seattle home overlooking the lake and was — where else — off to Disneyland. After the side trip to spend some time with his family, Darrell turned east toward Texas at an anxious, brisk clip.

After a speeding ticket in Arizona, Darrell and the family arrived in Dallas, where he glad-handed for a couple of days at the Cotton Bowl festivities. TCU defeated Syracuse, 28-27, on New Year's Day in one of the classic's all-time great games, and finally, Royal would be off for Austin. There he was soon in for both shock at the lack of first-class facilities and surprise at the unexpected preponderance of talent that he inherited.

And perhaps momentarily in the days before he rolled up his sleeves and went to work, Royal came to grips with the enormous task at hand in succeeding at a job he knew would either make or break his coaching career.

"I knew it was a good job, I knew the reason why I wanted it and I knew the ingredients were there to succeed. But I don't think I really knew how big a job it was until I got out and looked at it from a distance.

"I didn't know how many pieces you are required to put together to make for a long coaching career at one

20 YEARS AT TEXAS

Year	W	L	T
1957	6	4	1
1958	7	3	0
1959	9	2	0
1960	7	3	1
1961	10	1	0
1962	9	1	1
1963	11	0	0
1964	10	1	0
1965	6	4	0
1966	7	4	0
1967	6	4	0
1968	9	1	1
1969	11	0	0
1970	10	1	0
1971	8	3	0
1972	10	1	0
1973	8	3	0
1974	8	4	0
1975	10	2	0
1976	5	5	1
Total	167	47	5

place. You've got to deal with the morale of the squad and the staff. You have to have the good will of the faculty and the administration. And you just have no idea how many alums are involved. You've got to know the political climate of the state, without actually getting involved, but you've got to be in tune.

"You've got to know the regents, yet not ever go to them for approval for anything at any time. You have to stay in the chain of command. Let the president make the decisions, because you can't circumvent the athletic council. And you've got to know who the doers and shakers are as far as athletics are involved."

But whatever problems he would encounter, Royal knew he had the basis for a long stay.

"Everything was there, it just needed some treatment. It's a great university in a big state right there in a great city that is the state capital and a great place to live. I knew I was there."

But there were immediate tasks at hand.

Though he didn't have to, Royal called a meeting of Ed Price's staff to tell them he was sorry that most of them were being dismissed, but that he was bringing in his own staff and he wished them well.

"He didn't have to do that," pointed out T. Jones, who was one of two coaches — Robert Schulze being the other — Royal kept off Price's staff. "But he faced those other coaches, wished them well and said he hoped they understood that he was bringing in his own people."

Royal invited Jones to take him to the airport and offered him a chance to stay in private.

His first staff at Texas consisted of Mike Campbell,

A jubilant Royal and his team celebrate the 19-12 win over Oklahoma in 1959.

Jim Pittman, Charley Shira, Ray Willsey, Jack Swarthout, Schulze and Jones. It was a close-knit bunch, far from the makeup of the previous unit.

"Just ideal," Royal said. "We had good morale, we all agreed on how to approach the game and I'd like to think we did some things right."

And though the facilities were a shock, Royal even turned that to his advantage early after hearing some of his assistants echo his concerns.

"They hadn't done anything around there in years apparently," Royal said. "The practice field was terrible, the facilities were bad and I didn't even have an office to myself. I'm not kidding when I tell you I had a metal chair that was literally held together by dirty black tape.

"We were all in this brick-walled office together and because I was new, the phone was ringing off the wall. My secretary (Blanche Rhodes, who was with him throughout his tenure at Texas) did the best she could, but there were times when I had to answer the phone while she was taking dictation and all my assistant coaches were also there trying to work."

Royal called a staff meeting.

John Lujack (left) and sports writer Blackie Sherrod congratulate Royal on being selected as Coach of the Year in 1961.

"I asked them what if we came in and everything was up to snuff just like we'd like it? Now where do you start to make improvement? All these things you're complaining about are the greatest encouragement we could have. We can't do it all over night; but in time, we'll get all these problems straightened out."

They started with brushes and cans of paint and painted the dressing rooms for the players. Then they set about killing the stickers on the practice field, and Royal wrangled a sprinkler system. Six years after Royal's arrival, the improvements were more noticeable to all — new coaching offices including a private office for himself, a new playing surface in Memorial Stadium and a

new practice field, new concession stands and parking facilities, a remodeled press box and an $80,000 lettermen's lounge. With more to come, beginning in 1967.

But during that initial sprucing-up period, Royal felt compelled to offer sound reasoning behind the expenditure.

"I want our athletes to dress right, travel right, eat good and stay at good places," he said. "Things like this must never be an issue. All these things sustain morale. I'm convinced the world is divided into winners and losers.

"I know what it's like to take those long bus trips to a game. Eat that box lunch. You pull into the big school's campus and its campus is prettier, the stadium's bigger, the dressing room is better. Your fans can talk it up all year, throw the backyard barbecue and sing the fight song. But that big school, they're not even thinking about you until a couple of days before the next game. Then they beat your fanny and forget about you until the game the next year."

Royal had things on his mind other than improving facilities and building a football team when he arrived in Austin shortly after the turn of 1957. He instituted a series of moves that would send the message that this young coach knew more than just the intricacies of the Split-T offense.

He started a program to knock down the barrier between academics and athletics by inviting three professors to be a part of home game weekends — which included sharing meals with the team on Friday night and pre-game Saturday, getting a sideline pass for the game and being in the dressing room before kickoff and at halftime.

And he also did something that he regards as his greatest legacy to college athletics.

"The thing I am most proud of is that I was the first to have a full-time academic counselor," Royal said. "Now, every major school in America has one."

The first was a mild-mannered high school science teacher from nearby Lockhart, the late Lan Hewlett.

"When I first got to Texas, I had people recommending that we hire a full-time recruiter, which no one else had. I entertained the idea, but I did a little study involving the freshman class of four years ago and I quickly resolved that the retention rate was bad. People were flunking out and moving on. So I went to the athletic council and said it looked like we had a retention problem, that no one was paying any attention to the student."

Royal noted that there was usually an assistant coach who was delegated to such duty, "but I told them it was a pain in the fanny to them — and it was only better than nothing. I told them I wanted to hire a purely academic person who was not even remotely interested in working his way into a coaching position. The council went for it in a heartbeat."

When Royal answered, he heard on the other end the deep, booming baritone voice of Dana X. Bible. Royal momentarily put his hand over the phone and said, "Edith, this is it. It's the University of Texas."

Royal asked for recommendations and council member O.B. Williams immediately brought up Hewlett's name. Royal called him, liked him and hired him.

"What a great recommendation," said Royal, who was very specific with his instruction for this ground-breaking position.

"I told Lan that I didn't want him spending a lot of time with the honor students, the ones who were going to get their work done. Not to deny help to good students, but I wanted him with the borderline guys, the guys who were teetering on the brink of leaving school. And I can't tell you how many kids over the years told me they couldn't have made it if not for Lan Hewlett."

Today, the national organization of academic counselors gives a Lan Hewlett Award at their national convention.

"All that has happened in that area since came from a seed that was planted with the hiring of Lan Hewlett," Royal said.

The seeds of his overall program thus planted, Royal and his staff now turned to football. And they discovered some good football players — led by backfield star Walter Fondren and a promising group of sophomores-to-be that included players such as Bobby Lackey, Mike Dowdle, Maurice Doke, Monte Lee, Max Alvis, Larry Stephens and others.

None of whom had ever heard of Darrell K Royal.

"He was unknown, particularly to the players," Bobby Lackey said. "I mean here's a 32-year-old guy who is only 10 years older than some of the players and his staff was all pretty young, too. And they were taking the place of a lot of older coaches.

"But he made an immediate impression. I remember him walking into the dressing room and just standing there. There were some people over in the corner jackin' around, but you could hear the silence spread. It was like, 'He's here. I don't know where the hell he is, but he's here.'"

CHAPTER SEVEN

The Building of a Dynasty

With Five Straight Winning Seasons, Royal & Co. Are Poised to Achieve Greatness

Ever the quarterback, Darrell Royal licked his fingertips and pulled Bobby Lackey in tight, straining to be heard with what was left of his voice over the incredible din of more than 75,000 fans packed into the Cotton Bowl — half of them wearing burnt orange and the other half a sea of red.

Both the Texas and Oklahoma band sections were full of youngsters with exhausted lungs and puffed Dizzy Gillespie cheeks as the sounds of *Texas Fight* and *Boomer Sooner* mingled in an almost indistinguishable brass cacophony punctuated by the gut-rumbling boom of bass drums and the rat-a-tat-tat of their timpani cousins.

Little more than three minutes remained in what had become yet another classic Texas-OU battle on a cool and cloudy October afternoon in Dallas in the fall of 1958.

The Longhorns, who at kickoff were 13-point underdogs to the No. 2-ranked Sooners, trailed, 14-8, with less than four minutes to play after Oklahoma defensive lineman Jim Davis had plucked a mishandled handoff off the hip of Texas fullback Mike Dowdle and bolted 24 yards for the go-ahead touchdown moments earlier.

After the kickoff, Royal had turned to backup quarterback Vince Matthews, who, as scout team quarterback running opposition plays, had a more limber arm than Lackey, who didn't pass much out of Royal's Split-T offense. Matthews responded, taking the Longhorns downfield with precision throws as Royal paced the sidelines like a caged cat, ever thinking one, two plays ahead.

Royal enjoys a victory ride after the Longhorns defeated Texas A&M, 13-3, in 1962.

Third and goal from the OU seven. A field goal would do Texas little good. Another passing down? Maybe, maybe not. The fact that Lackey was now coming into the game put the Oklahoma defenders in a quandary, which was what Royal was counting on. Few knew before the snap that Royal was sending in the 6-foot-3 Lackey to throw a jump pass — a shoe for which Royal had been seeking a foot much of the afternoon. This was the fit for which he'd been waiting, a play with which he had been successful as the quarterback for the team across the way.

"Vince had done a great job," Royal later explained, "but Lackey is a big, tall boy and I wanted somebody who could see over the Oklahoma line. I'd wanted to send in that play (which he had used only once that season) earlier because their middle linebacker was in tight. I was afraid they would change their defense before we could use it. I was hoping they'd keep (their defense) the same, and they did. With Lackey in, I thought they might expect a run."

"They were in a gap-eight defense," Lackey remembered. "It left the end wide open."

At the snap, Lackey moved right down the line, then jumped up and threw back to end Bob Bryant, all alone in the end zone behind stunned Sooner defenders. The Texas half of the Cotton Bowl went berserk as Old Smokey, the cannon, blew a 10-gauge silver smoke ring toward the south end zone scoreboard, which showed 3:10 left in the struggle.

Lackey then kicked the point-after for a 15-14 Texas lead over the unbeaten Sooners, who had won 52 of their last 53 games and seen their monumental 47-game winning streak snapped only the season before by Notre Dame.

But as happened so many times during Royal's 20-year stint on the Texas sideline, the defense would have to

73

make a stand. With 70 seconds left, Lackey came up with the game-saving interception.

Texas had broken Oklahoma's six-year string of victories, as Royal had promised the Longhorns would at his hiring two years before.

Afterward, the professor greeted the former pupil at midfield.

"You beat us bad," Wilkinson said. "You beat us a lot worse than a 15-14 score would show."

A picture in Sunday's Daily Oklahoman would show Wilkinson covering his eyes with his left hand as he addressed reporters later outside the OU dressing room.

But as dusk settled over the grounds, bringing to life the brilliant colored lights of the State Fair of Texas, orange-wearing Longhorn fans streamed into the evening with 'Hook-em Horns' extended high while sportswriters up in the Cotton Bowl press box furiously clacked away at their portable typewriters pulling out each completed page and holding it aloft — where a Western Union runner patrolling the area would snatch it — before rolling in another copy-paper sandwich, with a carbon slice in the middle.

Several seized on the recent Pioneer rocket launch — the latest in a series of catch-up moves by the United States to overcome the Soviet lead in the Cold War space race — for analogy.

Bill Rives, the sports editor of The Dallas Morning News, wrote:

"If the Pioneer finally projects itself to the moon, it will find that it didn't arrive first.

"The University of Texas football team is already there. The Longhorns flashed to the moon Saturday afternoon in the Cotton Bowl, where they came from behind to score the grandest victory in the modern memory of their supporters."

But it was left to the immortal Blackie Sherrod, Rives' counterpart at The Dallas Times-Herald, to capture the fire and passion of the moment.

"A twisting, clawing Texas team fought Oklahoma lightning with brilliant aerial bolts of its own brand, bursting the proud Sooner bubble with a 15-14 explosion in the quivering Cotton Bowl.

"The furious Longhorns broke a bitter, six-year in-

Bud Wilkinson (left) diagrams a play for LSU's Paul Deitzel and Royal at a Look magazine dinner in 1962.

terstate drought to sweet smithereens with three minutes of clutch dramatics in the last quarter — a jagged touchdown journey that left 76,000 screaming citizens on the brink of a mass coronary."

Bedlam reined in the Texas dressing room.

"No team ever gave a coach so much to be happy about," Royal said amidst the mob scene. "They all played inspired and I'll tell you, when every man is fired up, you can catch a faster man. A fired-up team can beat a team with better material."

Soon thereafter few teams would be able to claim better material than the ones Royal fielded. And though his celebrated third-down move was perhaps the first widely acclaimed roll of the dice, it would by far not be his last.

"He just had a feel for the game," Lackey said in retrospect. "I think the same kind of thing happened in the 1969 game against Arkansas when he let (James) Street throw that pass. He had a feel and they all certainly didn't work out, but I think his record speaks for itself."

That 1958 victory over Oklahoma — the first of eight in a string that would stretch to 12 of 13 before a slide in the 1970's — was monumental in establishing Royal's program.

"More than any one single game in my coaching career, that established the fact that we could compete and were for real," Royal reflected. "That game — more than any other game maybe — established that I was a head coach for real."

It certainly was the high point of Royal's second season. On the strength of that win, Texas vaulted to No. 4 in the Associated Press rankings — the highest national regard for a Texas team since 1951 — before tumbling to SWC powers Rice, SMU and TCU and a 7-3 record.

But following a surprising 6-4-1 showing that included a second-place finish in the SWC and a Sugar Bowl loss to powerful No. 7 Mississippi, there now could be little doubt about Texas' decision to hire its youngest coach in a football history dating back to 1893.

"I think the Oklahoma game and the last game of the season the year before (1957) when we beat Texas A&M (9-7) were the games that turned the program around," said Lackey, who now runs a produce farming business in the Valley.

"A&M had a hell of a football team that year. John David Crow won the Heisman Trophy and that was Bear Bryant's last regular-season game (before moving to Alabama). I just think that Darrell and his staff just out-coached Bear Bryant that day. They had more talent than we did, but Darrell and his coaches had us more prepared."

Lackey's observation is an oft-repeated refrain, echoed by players of each generation in Royal's career at Texas. And it was evident from those early days that no one was going to outwork this young coach with boundless energy.

"When I really knew that Darrell had something was when I'd go by there and he'd be rumbling around at five o'clock in the morning and would stay until late at night," noted Rooster Andrews, an early riser himself.

"He never missed a trick, learning everything there was to know. He might have made some mistakes, but he was trying. And he could say things to those players, make those guys jump, get reaction from them that nobody else could."

Andrews was not alone in soon picking up on that Royal trait in those early days.

"He worked as hard as any coach I've ever met. But the thing that Darrell probably did best in my mind was motivate the individual and the team collectively to play a game on Saturday about as well as anybody I've ever seen," said T. Jones, one of the assistant coaches from the Ed Price regime.

Royal and Alabama's Paul (Bear) Bryant visit prior to the 1960 Bluebonnet Bowl game.

"There were a lot of coaches who probably knew as much or more about the game than Darrell did at the time, but his real key was the ability to communicate to the athlete his vigor and enthusiasm."

And he did it in different ways, seldom ranting to make his point. Seeming to always know just what touch to use. Jones pulled from his memory one instance in the third game of the 1958 season in Memorial Stadium against Texas Tech.

He and Royal happened to be walking off the field together after pre-game drills when Tech's mounted masked rider thundered past on a huge, black horse.

"He just missed us by inches," Jones said. "I mean he almost ran over us.

"So we get into the dressing room and it was a long

Royal and sports writer pal Blackie Sherrod sign copies of the book, "Darrell Royal Talks Football."

his approach to bowl games — lightening the workout load a little — after putting his team through tough two-a-day practices in full pads before the Sugar Bowl on New Year's Day 1958, where they fell, 39-7, to a more talented Ole Miss team.

But even today, Royal scoffs at the idea his team lost that day because he worked them too hard. And even yet, he was a step ahead, as usual.

"We worked too hard? They were worn out? Well, that's not true," he said. "They were young. We just got beat. They had their legs. But I tried to make another spring practice out of it. I was looking ahead to the next year."

Though tough in his approach to the game, Royal even then left no doubt that he would back his players all the way.

time before Darrell came in to address the squad. Everyone was getting a little anxious, wondering where he was. But he finally came in and said, 'Men, let me tell you something. I don't have much to tell you about offense or defense at this point. But I will tell you this. Watch out for that damn black horse or he'll run over you.'"

Texas won a hard-fought 12-7 victory that afternoon in a prelude to the historic struggle with Oklahoma the next Saturday.

From the opening of those first, hard-nosed days of spring training in early 1957, Royal got across the message that only the strong would survive to play for him. He mixed his more-talented sophomores in with the less-gifted, but equally determined upperclassmen to form a tough, cohesive team.

"I don't think anyone fully realized how many good sophomores we inherited," Royal said. "Tough, hard-nosed, dedicated players. We pushed them and they responded. As seniors, they took us to our first Cotton Bowl."

And along the way, Royal was still learning. He changed

In those days, managers put fan mail for the players in their lockers, or on the bench where they would find them when they came in for the afternoon's practice. One afternoon, Lackey found a telegram that was especially critical of him when he was only reflecting Royal's conservative style of play — which included frequent quick-kicks on third down, a fond tool in Royal's field-position chess game.

Lackey usually chunked critical letters as most players do. But because it was a telegram and the sender called him "gutless" among other things, he showed it to the head coach after practice. Royal read the telegram and he got that familiar steel-eyed, set-jaw look.

"Come on," he said to Lackey, and headed for his office, ordering Lackey to sit while he picked up the phone, called information and then put in a call to the sender — whose origin was listed on the telegram form.

"He called that guy and proceeded to eat him out," Lackey said. "He said, 'Don't you ever send one of my players a telegram again. If you've got something to say, you say it to me or send it to me; but don't be sending it to my players because they do what I say do. They're my players.'

"Boy, that made me feel great. I mean, here's this guy

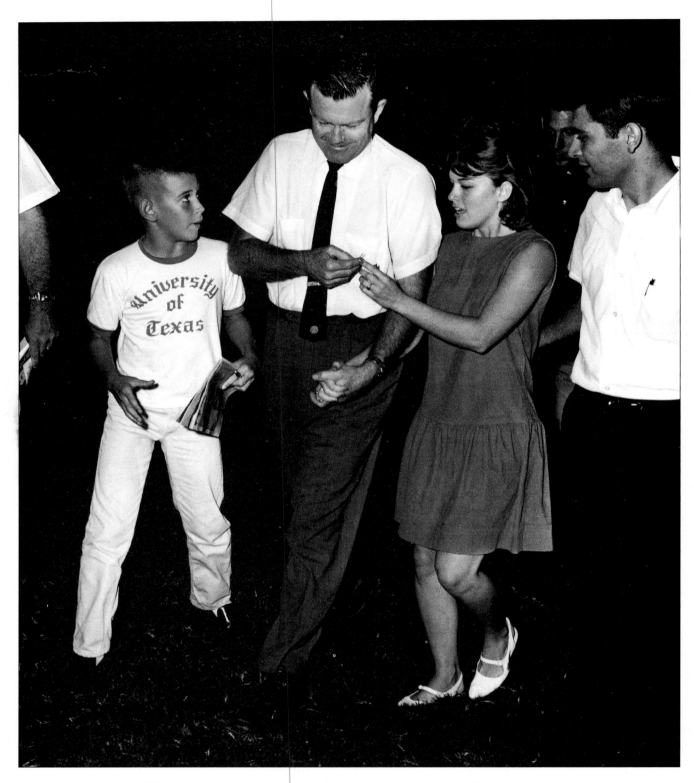

After a Texas game in 1962, Royal gets an escort from the field by his daughter, Marian.

taking up for me with me sitting right there. He didn't say he would take care it. He did it right then and there with me in the room. I certainly had a lot of respect for him after that."

Soon the nation was to have respect for Royal's program.

Texas roared to nine victories in 10 regular-season games and a Southwest Conference tri-championship in 1959, losing only to TCU (14-9), a team that would later prove an even bigger nemesis.

Royal lost, 23-14, to national champion Syracuse in his first Cotton Bowl game as a coach — a game sparked by a small mid-field brawl and charges of dirty play leveled against Texas players and racism against both the Longhorns and the city of Dallas. Reminiscent of similar remarks when Syracuse had played in the Orange Bowl the year before, the flurry of comment soon died and was forgotten.

Texas was 7-3-1 in 1960, including a 3-3 tie with Alabama in the Bluebonnet Bowl. But change was in the wind, both in the dawning of what would be a troubled decade for America and in the Texas offense.

In the summer of 1961, Royal decided to abandon his treasured Split-T in favor of what would become known as the "Flip-Flop" offense, which featured a scatback named James Saxton. Royal once said that Saxton ran like small-town gossip and that you could throw a handful of rice at him and miss. Frank Broyles in rare, colorful analogy, said he ran like a knuckleball.

It was the first time — but not the last — that Royal showed the inclination to tailor his offense to fit his personnel, not the reverse. The formation got its name from the fact that one side of the offensive line — after unfurling quickly from the huddle — always lined up on the strong side of the formation with the wingback, the first of which was Jack Collins. One of the keys to making it work was a hard-nosed quarterback named Mike Cotten, who was one of the best blockers on the team.

But there was no question that the converted 160-pound quarterback James Saxton was the reason behind the Flip-Flop offense, which would propel the Longhorns to 46 victories over the next five seasons

despite having as its base only a half-dozen plays run either right or left.

In 1961, the Texas offense gained 3,831 yards as compared to 2,500 the year before. Saxton and backups Jerry Cook and Tommy Ford finished first, third and seventh, respectively, in the SWC rushing totals. Saxton's average per carry rose from 5.4 yards per carry as a junior to an eye-opening 7.9 as he gained a Texas-record 849 yards while playing less than half the time — leading one writer to observe that he was the best back in the country who might not play enough to letter.

"We had a bunch of great tailbacks," pointed out Saxton, who is now an Austin banker. "I think Coach Royal was looking for the opportunity to use them more and some of it was me."

But even though Saxton was the focal point of the offense, Royal never let him overshadow the team.

Cotten recalls that in offensive film sessions, Royal seldom mentioned Saxton, other than from time to time to mumble, "Nice run."

"In about nine of the 10 games we played, James would break a long run, but he would hardly receive a mention from Coach Royal," Cotten said. "What he focused on were the blocks in the line that opened the holes and the downfield blocks. He would really applaud the blockers. And of course, me being primarily a blocker, I got a lot of applause and I thought it was great.

"And Saxton, you wouldn't even know he played in the damned game. But we all knew it was a team game and that it took 11 people to make it work. And James understood that as much as anybody."

Royal never missed an opportunity to keep his players motivated to excel beyond perceived limits.

"I remember one day three-quarters of the way through the (1961) season," Saxton said, smiling at the memory. "He called me in and said, 'James, you're gonna have to start getting with it. If you don't, we've got several boys that want to take your place.'

"I couldn't figure it out. I was gaining about 100 yards a game, I was making these long runs and I thought I was having a pretty good season."

So puzzled was Saxton that he did something he rarely did. He cut his next class and went back to his dorm room to find Cotten, his roommate, there.

"I walked in and Mike immediately asked me what was wrong. I told him what had happened and Mike started laughing. He said, 'That son of a gun. He did the same thing to me.' He just wanted to keep us on our toes."

Texas stormed through eight games of 1961 unbeaten, the closest score a 28-7 victory over Oklahoma. Then came the ninth game against TCU, which the Longhorns had managed to defeat, only 3-2, in 1960 but were 24-point favorites that day.

Saxton is lucky. He is one of the few who does not remember what ranks as one of Royal's most bitter defeats — the 6-0 loss that cost Texas its first possible national championship. After taking a short pass 45 yards, he was knocked out in the first quarter on a controversial hit by Bobby Plummer and did not return.

"We missed a couple of national championships by the skin of our teeth (including 1964) and we won a couple by the skin of our teeth," Royal said. "But that loss to TCU in 1961 stung."

It would sting again in later years because of the famous quip that was used over and over to fire up the Frogs for the Texas game.

"They're like a bunch of cockroaches," Royal said of the Horned Frogs. "It's not what they eat and tote off, it's what they fall into and mess up that hurts."

Royal said he only meant that TCU should have loftier ambitions than ruining Texas' season, but the intent was lost.

Nevertheless, Texas got back on track and smoked the Aggies, 25-0, on Thanksgiving Day to tie for its second SWC crown and qualify for its second Cotton Bowl game against No. 5 Ole Miss, where once again Royal's razor-sharp mind was key to a 12-7 victory.

"That was another time Coach Royal reached into his pocket and pulled out something that worked against a team that outweighed us by 40 pounds a man," Saxton noted. "I didn't carry the ball very much that day. He put me in motion and they pulled their linebackers out to cover me. Mike Cotten ran the option (with fullback Ray Poage or Collins) most of the day and Mike got most valuable player in the game."

Cotten agreed about Royal's game plan.

"Coach Royal was not the emotional type in the locker-room atmosphere; he was real business-like," Cotten said. "But as far as a strategist, some of the things that he put in before games we played are the reasons we won. We never would have beaten Ole Miss in the Cotton Bowl without some of the plays he put in.

"The first play we ran, I think, they stuffed us for a three-yard loss and I'm thinking that this was going to be a long day with our regular offense. But those little wrinkles he put in were the difference. It was just amazing. Every week there was something new and a lot of times that's what proved to be the difference in the ball game."

And again, Mike Campbell's defense stood tall. Jerry Cook had three crucial interceptions. Through Royal's first five seasons, the Longhorns put together 21 goal-line stands inside their 10-yard line where teams failed to score — saving at least nine games won by less than a touchdown.

Texas got a whiff of the national championship race for which its fans so longed during the 1961 season. But before the sweet smell of ultimate success, there would be tragedy and criticism to weather in 1962.

August and September of that year were unusually hot and muggy, and these were the days before the temperature/humidity index warned of danger. Within a week, SMU player Mike Kelsey and Texas' Reggie Grobb died after falling out during practice. Grobb's loss hit Royal harder than anything he had yet known in his adult life and would not know until a decade later when his daughter was killed in a traffic accident.

And it was in 1962, when Royal assumed a dual role as Texas' athletic director, that he heard discouraging words from the press and Longhorn fans spoiled by victory and angered over his conservative strategy. The first rumbling was the telegram back in 1958, and it reached a crescendo after a 14-14 tie with Rice that knocked Texas out of the No. 1 ranking after thrilling-but-close victories over Oklahoma (9-6) and Arkansas (7-3).

Against Rice, Royal twice elected to punt at near midfield on fourth-and-short yardage. Secondly, Rice coach Jess Neely elected to kick the tying point in the fourth quarter rather than go for two points and a possible monumental outcome, then sat on the ball when he got it back in the final minute. Texas nevertheless

The Royals enjoy an evening in Dallas with Mickey Mantle and his wife, Merlin, and the Wynnes in 1962.

won its first outright SWC championship before falling to LSU in the Cotton Bowl, 13-0.

Royal best answered his critics in two articles that followed — once in an April column by The Dallas Morning News' Gary Cartwright and again in talking to Dan Jenkins for his 1963 *Sports Illustrated* college football forecast.

"I admit I'm a conservative," Royal told Cartwright. "I think my conservative ideas have been exaggerated and maybe I've helped exaggerate them by playing the role, but I'm a conservative coach and I don't mind people saying it. Is there anything wrong with the label?

"I read all the things people write and it's clever. I see that I'm called the Barry Goldwater of college football, and I notice that I've invented the quick, quick kick and I laugh when I see somebody like Bud Shrake write that if you want to see somebody really nervous look at Darrell Royal when he suddenly realizes it's

third down and his team still has the ball.

"That's funny. I know it's exaggerated but you have to laugh."

He took a somewhat different slant with Jenkins.

"Sure, we're in the entertainment business, and as an athletic director, I can see that it would be good to open up our game a little. But as a coach, I can assure you that nothing is as entertaining as winning ... We have neglected the pass and we'll work harder on that. But we'll do it because we think it'll help us win, not because it's better showbiz."

As a footnote, it should be noted that Duke Carlisle threw four touchdown passes in the Longhorns' Orange & White spring game. And though Royal didn't necessarily get pass-happy during the 1963 season, not until the end of the decade would Longhorn fans find a season more entertaining. Because Texas won. And they won 'em all.

CHAPTER EIGHT

A Season to Remember

A Team Loaded with Talent and a Pair of Battles
Between No. 1 and No. 2 Frame a Memorable Year in the Sun

Edith Royal remembers trying to console all-American linebacker Johnny Treadwell after the 6-0 loss to TCU in 1961 that knocked Texas out of the No. 1 ranking and eventually cost them their first best shot at the national championship.

"He walked right by me," Edith said. "But he did the same thing to his mother."

Added Darrell, "I felt the same way."

But resolve was born out of the disappointment of defeat that day in the hearts of an exceptional group of young players, who like Treadwell shunned family and friends as dusk came to Austin that evening.

Sophomores David McWilliams and Tommy Ford declined offers from their parents to soak up their disappointment with a sizzling steak at Hill's Restaurant, seeing their families off for home before walking up the hill from Memorial Stadium to the athletic dorm.

Neither felt like eating, which was certainly unusual for young men their age. They didn't much feel like going to their rooms, either.

"Ford and I just sat there on the steps of Moore Hill Hall and we made a pact," McWilliams remembered. "We said that when we were seniors, we weren't going to let something like that happen again. I remember that very plainly. That's how strong that loss was.

"I've always thought that of the years I was there (1961-63), that the 1961 team was the most talented. After that, I think we won more games based on heart and

Royal, Douglas MacArthur and Texas Regent Wells Madden admire the MacArthur Bowl trophy.

having to win than we did on talent."

Perhaps McWilliams underestimates his own recruiting class that came to be referred to as "the Carlisle bunch," second only in Texas annals to "the Worster bunch" that came in toward the end of the decade and helped propel the Longhorns to another national championship and a 30-game winning streak. Only that later group was more productive than the 15 seniors who finished their eligibility in 1963 with only two regular-season losses in three seasons. Included were Carlisle, McWilliams, Ford, Scott Appleton, Tommy Wade and Charley Talbert.

"Recruiting wasn't such a big deal in those days as it is today," McWilliams said. "We (at Cleburne) were in the same district with Carlisle (at Athens), so I had heard of him before. But it wasn't like we all got together and said, 'Let's all go to Texas.' The first I became aware of how much talent was in our class was when I reported to the (THSCA) North-South All-Star camp and discovered there were about 20 or 25 players there who were going to Texas.

"When I started practicing with and against those guys, we all began to think about what a great bunch of athletes were going to school down there. So I think the excitement of our group started in the summer before we reported."

The resolve forged among that group of sophomores in 1961 was rekindled two years later as the now seniors-to-be left for the summer, still smarting over the 13-0 loss to LSU in the Cotton Bowl following another near-miss (9-0-1) season in 1962.

"We had all experienced the crushing disappointment of 1961 when we were so close to a national championship, and I think by the time we were seniors, we really wanted to make it through the season undefeated," said Carlisle, who emerged that spring as the No. 1 quarterback and a team leader along with McWilliams.

"But there were two things that came out of the LSU loss. One, that we had to work to prove that we were better than that. And the second thing we learned from the year before is that not only do you have to work to be better, you have to play every minute at 100 percent no matter who the opponent is. And not do anything foolish or make any slip-ups that could cost a game.

"Everybody knew that it is hard to go through a season undefeated, even if you have some supposedly weak teams on your schedule. You've got to be at your best and not let anyone slip up on you. So I think everyone went into that year with a real determination."

By the summer of 1963, many looked at Texas as a team that would contend for the national championship. Dan Jenkins picked the Longhorns in his annual *Sports Illustrated* preview, but Royal wasn't convinced.

"I felt like we were solid. We had a good offensive team and a good defensive team, and I felt like we had a chance of doing good," he said. "But a national championship team? No."

For one of the few times in his career, Royal — who closed pre-season practice sessions for the first time — was wrong. Though it appeared several times that he was right.

"You know," said Tommy Nobis, who as a sophomore moved into Treadwell's slot at middle linebacker that season, "that whole year I would have to say was meant to be. Because there were so many times when it looked like it wasn't."

Include a season-opening 21-0 victory over Tulane, a team that hadn't won a game in two years as the first of those times. But the Longhorns got rolling after that and blasted Texas Tech (49-7) and Oklahoma State (34-7), along the way rising from No. 5 in the season-opening Associated Press poll to No. 2 as they steamed into the annual Dallas showdown with Oklahoma.

The Sooners were riding even higher. They had taken out 1962 national champion and No. 1-ranked Southern California, 17-12, in Los Angeles in the second game of the season — after which lineman Ralph Neeley told a national television audience, "Texas is next."

But despite an open date before the Texas game, Oklahoma was not prepared for the buzzsaw it would encounter on that hot October afternoon with yet another national television audience looking on.

"We had seen them play on television against Southern Cal, and we all knew they were an outstanding team and that this was a huge game for us," Carlisle said.

Once again, Royal proved to be a strategic step ahead of the competition.

"We went to a tight slot with the wingback inside just slightly split," he said. "That put a little different look to the guy (on defense) who has to play that double-team. Sometimes, we had the wingback posting and the end drive. Other times, the end posted and the wingback went with the drive block. I felt like that little thing would help spring the pitchback."

It did. Royal did something else, too.

"We hadn't been running the old Split-T option in the prior years," Carlisle noted. "But we put it in for that game."

McWilliams remembered, "It was like they didn't even know how to defense it. We had a whole lot of success with Duke running that option."

Which didn't surprise Carlisle. He kept on the option six times for 37 yards as Texas stormed 68 yards with the opening kickoff to its first touchdown and consumed almost half the first quarter in doing it.

Also using the inside handoff to the hard-nosed Ford and the occasional power sweep, Carlisle scored the first TD on fourth and one. The Longhorns were off to a 21-0 lead — scoring in each of the first three quarters — as the defense stifled running back Joe Don Looney, limiting him to only four yards in six carries in a shocking 28-7 victory.

"I've always said the most impressive thing about Coach Royal was that I thought he was a genius at organization and preparation," said Carlisle, now in the oil and gas exploration business in Mississippi.

"I never went into a game and felt like the other team was better prepared than we were. Which obviously gives you a lot of confidence. You figure if you go out there and

Blackie Sherrod (left) and Look's Tim Cohane present Royal with the Grantland Rice award.

Royal chats with NBC-TV broadcaster Curt Gowdy at a pre-season luncheon in New York City.

do your job, you will win the game; or at least you are un-likely to lose it because of a stupid mistake or mental error.

"I think he just had an ability to have you ready to do what you needed to do against the opponent you were playing. And that came from his knowing them so well."

After his team was embarrassed in the first meeting between the nation's No. 1 and No. 2 teams since 1946 when Army and Notre Dame battled to a 0-0 tie, Oklahoma coach Bud Wilkinson called his team's effort "the poorest in the 17 years I have been head coach."

Again, Blackie Sherrod of The Dallas Times-Herald captured the moment.

"There was a scant two minutes left on the clock when the deafening jungle chant crashed down into the Cotton Bowl echo chamber: 'We're No. 1. We're No. 1'

"It was the only time Texas was late all afternoon.

"The Longhorn rooters could have started their boasting broadside much, much earlier in this latest chapter of magnificent lunacy. They didn't have to wait until

their furious heroes had battered their way to a 28-7 win over Oklahoma in this meeting of the country's two leading football teams.

"It was apparent almost from the opening kickoff, when Darrell Royal's Orange infantry grabbed OU's No. 1 ranking and flang it eagerly in the Sooner face."

After that game, Royal's players knew their dream had a real chance of coming true as they vaulted to the No. 1 ranking.

"We had talked about winning a national championship before," McWilliams said. "We knew we still had some tough games coming up, like Arkansas, but after we beat Oklahoma, we knew we really had a chance."

And Royal, in his post-game remarks, didn't miss a chance to take a jab at his critics who wanted him to get out of his unimaginative offense and chunk the football.

"We didn't pass much," Royal said with deadpan expression. "I hope nobody gripes too much about it."

Texas threw only three passes against OU. Two came in

the fourth quarter by sophomore quarterback Marvin Kristynik, who had the lone completion to George Sauer for 14 yards and the final Texas touchdown with 51 seconds left.

On the night before, on the same Cotton Bowl turf, SMU had upset No. 4 Navy, 32-28. On Saturday night, Baylor surprised Arkansas, 14-10, in its Southwest Conference opener as quarterback Don Trull completed 21 of 34 passes for 241 yards — and two touchdowns to his favorite receiver, soon-to-be all-American Lawrence Elkins.

Texas motored into Little Rock the next weekend and stormed to a 17-0 lead against the Razorbacks, but were forced to hold on as linebacker Ronnie Caveness led a second-half defensive stand and quarterback Jon Brittenum passed the Hogs back into the game. But Texas' defense again saved the day with some hard-nosed tackling as linebacker Timmy Doerr recovered two late fumbles.

Royal's teams had now beaten Arkansas five of six times, and for the first time since Frank Broyles became head coach, his team had lost two SWC games in a row.

With Arkansas now out of the way, most Longhorn fans assumed their team would not have to break a sweat the rest of the season. They were wrong. Rice, which helped spoil Texas' bid for national honors with that infamous 14-14 tie the season before, scared the pants off a Memorial Stadium sellout crowd of 65,530 the next week before falling, 10-6.

That had been the score since halftime, but nervous Texas fans were heartened as Carlisle directed a time-eating drive of almost nine minutes in the fourth quarter and thought the game was well in hand when Hix Green banged into the middle for two yards on fourth and one from the Owls' 9-yard line. But Green was thrown back for a yard loss on the next play. And then Carlisle threw an incompletion before being hit and momentarily knocked loose from the ball before recovering for a 12-yard loss.

Tony Crosby came on to attempt what looked like a gimme field goal. But Rice linebacker Russell Wyatt roared in to block the kick. End John Sylvester scooped it up, and it's likely that only a shoe-grabbing tackle by holder Joe Dixon at the 39-yard-line prevented Sylvester from scoring.

Rice quarterback Ben Hollingsworth quickly passed for 11 yards and a first down at midfield. He threw deep, but Anthony King batted the ball away at the UT 15.

Hollingsworth went deep again, but this time Dixon — who had thwarted a second-quarter drive with an interception — came up with his second key theft of the night, running it out of the end zone to the six.

From there, Carlisle ran out the clock.

"Man, we had a tough time with Rice," McWilliams said.

Texas had a tough time the next week before slipping past SMU, 17-12. The Longhorns scored on the opening drive for the sixth consecutive game, but then had to rely on numerous Mustang miscues for their other points. And Texas had to sweat out the final minutes again as SMU rallied with a fourth-quarter drive that culminated on Billy Gannon's diving catch for a 22-yard touchdown off the arm of sophomore quarterback Mac White with 5:57 to play.

But the Longhorn defense was there, stopping a running play for the two-point conversion that would have pulled the pass-happy Ponies within a field goal of upsetting the nation's No. 1 team. That afternoon, Navy blitzed Notre Dame, 35-14.

And so Texas and Baylor rolled into their Nov. 9 game in Austin with matching 4-0 conference records. The 5-1 Bears were unranked because of low pre-season regard and a 22-15 loss to Oregon State in the second game of the year. But behind the Trull-to-Elkins passing combination, they had knocked off SWC foes Arkansas, Texas Tech (21-17), Texas A&M (34-7) and TCU (32-13).

Baylor came into the game with added incentive, fueled by comments Royal had made to Jenkins for that pre-season article in *SI*, in which Royal talked about the necessity for first-class facilities.

"You hear guys who went to another school in our conference — A&M, Baylor or somewhere — talk for 20 minutes about why they didn't want to go to Texas. But you'll never hear a Longhorn explaining why he didn't go to another school.

"Put me in a room with 50 people and tell me half of them went to Texas. I'll sort 'em out. The guy with the blue, serge suit with his green socks rolled down didn't go to Texas."

Baylor coach John Bridgers, a man with a sense of humor, wore a blue suit with green socks on the sideline that gray November afternoon in Memorial Stadium, where there was more serious business afoot.

Trull connected with Elkins for 34 yards as the Bears launched an opening drive of 68 yards to a fourth down at the Longhorns' 12-yard line. Bridgers disdained the field-goal attempt. But Elkins overthrew end James Ingram in the end zone. Later, he reflected, "We had a chance to score on our first possession ... but then we didn't see the ball again until the fourth quarter."

Pretty close to the truth. After Baylor stopped the Longhorns' game-opening drive for the first time in the season, the Bears again moved into Texas territory. But this time Timmy Doerr jarred the ball loose from fullback Dalton Hoffman at the UT 23 and King recovered.

Incredibly, from that point on, Baylor's offense owned the ball for six plays and less than four minutes in the second and third quarters. And although Texas moved the ball, it wasn't until late in the third quarter that the Longhorns were able to cash in a scoring drive.

Texas took over at the Baylor 45 after a personal-foul penalty on a punt return. With Ford pounding into the line behind blocks from McWilliams, Nobis, George Brucks and Staley Faulkner; Texas marched downfield to face fourth and one at the Baylor four-yard line.

Crosby had missed a 12-yard field-goal attempt after a Texas probe reached the six in the second quarter. This time the call went to Ford — who gained a tough 101 yards on 27 carries that day. He bulled his way inside the 1-yard line, then sophomore fullback Tommy Stockton scored with 1:55 left in the third quarter.

Aided by a pass interference penalty, Baylor finally mounted one last drive from its 13 after a Stockton fumble late in the fourth quarter. Killing the clock by spiking the ball and expertly hitting first one, then another, receiver, Trull moved the Bears to the UT 19-yard line with 29 seconds left.

Defensive coordinator Mike Campbell screamed into his headset microphone from the press box to put Carlisle in at safety, where he had been a standout in 1962 but had not played that season.

Trull dropped back, looking for Elkins in the face of a four-man rush.

"Part of the responsibility of rushing Trull was for our guys to jam the tight end (Ingram), who was my responsibility on that play," Carlisle recalled.

"Charley Talbert really came down on him and made it difficult for (Ingram) to get off the line of scrimmage. When I saw that, I knew he wasn't going to be involved. I looked at Trull and saw he was looking toward the end zone, so I took off back that way."

Elkins, trying to shake Dixon, made a cut that gained him a step. And as he crossed the end line smack between the goal posts, he flashed open.

"I later saw one of the pictures taken from the end zone and it looked like I wasn't going to get there," Carlisle said. "That's always been so interesting to me because I remember feeling like I was there in plenty of time. I was worried about having the ball tipped and making sure Elkins didn't reach back over me and catch it."

Neither Trull nor Elkins remembers seeing Carlisle in the picture until he leapt and snatched the ball out of the air before it reached Elkins over his inside shoulder.

"We really didn't jostle for it," Carlisle said. "His momentum carried him one way and mine carried me another.

"It's interesting how a second or two can play out. You think of the weirdest things. I guess being the quarterback and knowing our day wasn't finished, I remember coming down with the ball and thinking that I was on our 1-yard line instead of in the end zone. I'm thinking, 'Oh, hell. I got to take another snap right down here on the goal line.' I was already thinking a play ahead."

Just like his coach. But Carlisle shuns the notion that his heroic interception was the only key to victory, though what Baylor might have done after a touchdown is conjecture.

"Baylor had one of the best passing attacks in the country. And that interception takes away from the fact that our defense held that offense scoreless for the entire afternoon," he said. "That in itself was remarkable."

And so the Longhorns survived Baylor. But the nail-biting was far from over. Texas cleared the TCU hurdle, 17-0, with another top defensive effort the next week. They were probably fortunate they had a week off before playing the annual Thanksgiving Day battle with Texas A&M. But maybe not.

That next week, President John F. Kennedy was assassinated in Dallas.

Kennedy had been scheduled to visit Austin for a dinner that night, where Royal was to present him with a football autographed by the nation's No. 1-ranked team.

"I didn't have a very good game against A&M," Carlisle said. "But it wasn't because my mind was somewhere else. Everybody was back focused on football by then."

The usual shenanigans, not uncommon at the time, were again afoot. Aggies kidnapped Bevo and in retaliation, some Texas students tried to burn Bevo's name into the Kyle Field playing surface with grass-killing chemicals. A&M groundskeepers covered the field with dirt and sprayed it green for the national TV audience. That plus a steady day-and-a-half rain contributed to make the field a quagmire.

Royal wasn't sure how his team was going to play. He couldn't sleep. He openly fretted about how Longhorn fans brushed off any suggestion that the Aggies could give Texas any kind of a game, afraid the team would catch the drift. He was concerned about how quiet his team was before kickoff and then he almost missed getting on the bus for the short drive to College Station.

It looked once again like the Longhorns might miss the bus to a national championship when A&M took a 13-3 lead in the second half. But Texas took advantage of a fumble to drive 35 yards to Ford's two-yard scoring run early in the fourth quarter, although Carlisle's two-point conversion pass was incomplete.

The Aggies missed what could have been a game-winning 52-yard field goal with just over five minutes left.

Center David McWilliams and UT quarterback Duke Carlisle huddle with Royal prior to the 1964 Cotton Bowl.

And as Royal had done when he turned to relief pitcher Vince Matthews against Oklahoma in 1958, he called on Tommy (The Rifleman) Wade to move his team downfield with the pass in one more desperate situation.

Wade hit five of 10 passes for 61 yards. One interception was fumbled away when an Aggie tried an open-field lateral on the return and another ruled an incompletion when the Aggie defender came down out of the back of the end zone. On his 10th pass, Wade connected with wingback Phil Harris for 13 yards to the one. A play later, Royal sent Carlisle back in. He dove in for the touchdown with 1:19 left, but slipped and fell in the mud coming away from center on a two-point conversion play.

Safety Jim Hudson's ensuing interception preserved the 15-13 victory and the first undefeated season for the Texas Longhorns since 1920.

Governor John Connally's wife, Nellie, called afterward to offer congratulations. Governor Connally, wounded in the attack that killed President Kennedy, was still in the hospital in Dallas. Mrs. Connally said she let the governor watch the game until he became too excited.

Meanwhile, the Cotton Bowl selection committee had announced it would not invite the visiting team until after the Army-Navy game on Nov. 30. The Midshipmen had crept back up to No. 2 in the nation after beating Michigan and Eastern power Pittsburgh and there was no doubt the committee wanted a 1-2 matchup — which would unfold on the Cotton Bowl turf for the second time in a memorable season.

CHAPTER NINE

The Battle for No. 1

The Longhorns, with a Corralling Defense and a Potent Aerial Attack Met Navy in the Cotton Bowl on New Year's Day

ormer Heisman Trophy winner and all-NFL quarterback Roger Staubach says there are only two losses from a long and distinguished playing career that bring him particular pain.

"The Texas game and the second time we lost to the Pittsburgh Steelers in the Super Bowl," he said. "(The Dallas Cowboys) could have been the first team to win three Super Bowls, but we lost, 35-31. And we could have won the national championship at Navy, which would have been the cap to a great year."

The Midshipmen lost that national 1963 championship bid to a totally dominant team from the University of Texas, 28-6, in the Cotton Bowl Classic.

"We had a heck of a football team that year," Staubach said. "We beat Notre Dame, Michigan and Pittsburgh, which lost only one game. But we ran into a machine that just was better than us.

"Texas was extremely well coached. Their defense and the Steelers' defense were the two best that I ever faced. Now, I'm not comparing the Texas defense to the Steelers, I'm just talking about the best defenses on their respective levels. Texas had a great plan that day."

Mike Campbell was a successful high school coach in Canton, Mississippi, when he first met Darrell Royal. Royal, the new, young head coach at Mississippi State, had stopped by to introduce himself and inquire about a couple of prospects. The two immediately struck up a cordial friendship, but nothing special.

All-America Tommy Nobis was the greatest linebacker in Longhorns' history.

"I remember he was a sharp-looking, young guy who loved to talk football," said Campbell, whose team had just won a state championship.

They saw each other infrequently over the next year. Once when Campbell visited spring practice, again at a coaching school and a couple of times the next season when Campbell would take a player or two to a game either there or to Ole Miss. But when Campbell heard Royal had taken the job at Washington, he called him to see if he had filled his new staff.

Royal told him no, but that he felt obligated to hire a high school coach from Washington state.

"But then later on he called back and said if I still wanted to go, the job was there," Campbell said. "I don't know if I thought then that he might be headed for bigger things, but I knew I wanted to be a college coach and this was better than what I was doing as a high school coach in Mississippi."

It was, as the saying goes, the beginning of a beautiful relationship.

"Mike is like family," Royal said. "And he had a big influence on my coaching. He was one heck of a football coach. He just had so much common sense and there's no better way to coach. He was always close to the players, and I knew I didn't have to worry about the defense with Mike.

"But Mike never hoarded players for defense. If he had someone down there he thought would help on offense, he'd say so. And he was just as quick to recommend something on offense as he did on defense. He was a team player."

And though Royal again came up with some wrinkles that proved pivotal in the offensive explosion of points against Navy in the Cotton Bowl victory, Campbell's defense and the now-famous Staubach Drill live on prominently in the lore surrounding the game.

"Rightly so," Royal said.

Campbell didn't worry so much about Staubach's ability to drop straight back and throw. It was his dangerous scrambling — with which Staubach terrorized the NFL during his career with the Cowboys — that worried him.

"Roger was a great football player," Campbell said. "But where he was killing everybody was when they would rush him, and he would come out of the pocket. Once he came out of that pocket, you had your hands full because it would take forever and a day to corral him."

Other coaches no doubt recognized the same thing. But there was a hidden key to Campbell's plan.

"Other people rushed Roger," Royal pointed out, "but Mike didn't let the guys rushing him to get out of their lanes. If this one chooses to go around this block and that one goes around his, that's just what Staubach wanted. Boom, he's through that opening and he's gone. So not only did Mike teach containment on the outside, he kept everyone in a lane."

"We decided that if Staubach was going to do any running around," Campbell said, "it was going to be towards his own goal line."

Thus the Staubach Drill was born. At the end of every practice, Campbell's instruction was put to grueling test. His defenders scrambled for long periods at a time to contain the scout team quarterback. And it took both Tommy Wade and Marvin Kristynik to play Staubach. One man would have fallen out trying to do it.

"They gave us some statistic that 80 percent of Staubach's passes had come after he had broken containment," said David McWilliams, who was an end on defense and a center offensively in the waning years of one-platoon football. "They preached containment every day. And at the end of every practice, we'd do the Staubach Drill instead of conditioning.

"We might go three, four minutes at a time. Our job was not to tackle the quarterback, but if he rolled away to keep getting deeper than he did while the other guys protected the middle. We did that until our tongues hung out.

"We lost containment only one time against Staubach in that game. I have to mention, though, that it was against the second unit."

Texas dropped the 1963 Heisman Trophy winner for 55 yards in losses and twice separated him from the foot-ball. Outland Trophy winner Scott Appleton was voted the game's most valuable lineman.

"The defensive ends told Scott we made him an all-American that day," McWilliams said. "Because we funneled him back into Appleton, and he made about every tackle."

Texas also stopped what had been a respectable Navy rushing attack, which ended the day with minus-14 yards. Staubach contends that might not have happened had not fullback Pat Donnelly pulled a hamstring in practice the week before. And, that wingback Phil Harris wouldn't have caught touchdown passes of 58 and 63 yards if Donnelly — the covering linebacker — had been 100 percent.

Maybe. Maybe not.

"It helped, but that was coincidental," Carlisle said of Donnelley's injury. "We had put in a new play (a pass option) involving Phil Harris before (Donnelly) got hurt. It had to do with something Coach Royal had spotted in their defense, and we attacked it successfully."

So successfully that Carlisle, the infantry quarterback, threw for a short-lived Cotton Bowl passing record 213 yards on seven completions before retiring to the bench in the third quarter. Staubach, who resorted to straight drop-back passes in the second half, later passed him with 228 yards. But he did not throw a touchdown pass.

Carlisle did leave with the Cotton Bowl total offense record of 267 yards. All the Navy men — including outspoken Middies' coach Wayne Hardin — and everyone else agreed with both final wire polls that Texas was indeed the best college football team in the country. By then the Longhorns already had the symbolic MacArthur Trophy safely in Austin.

"It was a special time," said Royal, the national coach of the year who had only one real disappointment. When General Douglas MacArthur presented the trophy named after him, former staff sergeant Duke Royal had hoped to talk a little military strategy with the retired general. But all MacArthur wanted to talk about was football.

The Navy game was the last of Carlisle's career. He, like Mike Cotten before him and James Street later, developed a sixth sense of what Royal wanted in the days before coaches called every play. He said he and Royal had a business-like relationship, but it was not without its wry, lighter moments, as Carlisle likes to recall.

Longhorns quarterback Duke Carlisle blistered Navy with a Cotton Bowl-record 267 yards total offense.

Once when he was a sophomore, he stepped into the open door of Royal's office one afternoon. Texas was to open the 1961 season against California in Berkeley. Carlisle had a friend who played for SMU and who had played on the West Coast the year before and done some sight-seeing. Carlisle mentioned this to Royal and said since they would be so close to San Francisco, a tour might be educational.

Carlisle said Royal never looked up from his desk. He asked what SMU's record was and Duke replied, 3-7.

"That's exactly right," Royal shot back. "That's not what I have in mind. See you at practice."

The next fall, Carlisle — who McWilliams said used to drive him nuts with his loosy-goosy attitude before games while McWilliams was stifling waves of nervous nausea — approached his coach with another idea. Sev-

eral players had noticed that Mississippi warmed up without pads before the 1962 Cotton Bowl (won by Texas, 12-7) and thought it might be an interesting concept.

"Coach Royal said he had no problem with that. Anybody willing to play without shoulder pads was certainly free to warm up without them."

Another time Carlisle and Royal were watching a game on TV together. The coach sent in a play, but the quarterback waved the messenger off and went with his own selection.

"I laughed and said, 'Coach, you probably wouldn't want me to do that, would you?' He said, 'Let me put it this way. If you ever wave one of mine away, the play you call had better score.' I decided I would just stick with his suggestions. I wasn't prepared to go with that much pressure."

CHAPTER TEN

Wishbone Magic

A Daring Innovation and a New Formation
Lead the Longhorns Back to the Top

If there was ever a time when Darrell Royal felt the heat of his job — any more than he constantly put upon himself — it was now as he nervously paced the sidelines awaiting the kickoff on an early October night against Oklahoma State in 1968.

"Hell, yes I was under a little pressure," Royal said. "Think about it. We'd had three 6-4 seasons in a row, and we tie our first game against Houston and lose the second to Texas Tech. So we weren't starting off too good. And I couldn't sleep. We were struggling."

Royal, who blamed himself for a drop-off in quality of recruiting depth following the 1963 national championship, had immersed himself even deeper into the task of restoring Texas' national luster that had dimmed after another outstanding season in 1964. That year had been tainted only by a 14-13 loss to Arkansas when a late two-point conversion try failed. The Razorbacks went on to defeat Nebraska in the Cotton Bowl, and Texas rebounded handsomely with one of its greatest-ever bowl victories — a 21-17 upset of then-No. 1 Alabama.

"Darrell would get discouraged from time to time," longtime aide Mike Campbell said. "But if he was down, he would fight even harder than he would if he was up. He fought. That was him."

Now feeling as though he was on the ropes for the first time in his coaching career, Royal had called into play any tool at his disposal.

"I got involved," he said. "The enthusiasm of the student body and just everybody had gotten down. So I really got involved in the pep rally before the Oklahoma State game. I mean we needed support. We needed somebody."

Or some thing. And though Royal had no way of knowing what was about to transpire that night, he then had in his arsenal a weapon that would prove more mighty than any other on college football's scene at the time. Royal had installed the Wishbone offense only during the preceding two-a-day practices but was poised to slide onto a track that would produce 30 consecutive victories, a piece of two more national titles and two of the greatest wins in Texas football history.

Royal had gone to the I-formation in the mid-1960's, but was not satisfied with the offense, despite the presence of two very talented athletes in quarterback Bill Bradley and I-back Chris Gilbert. The Longhorns worked out of the "I" during spring training. Royal still had a problem with it despite a spectacular spring game from Bradley, who had shaken off knee problems from the previous season.

This was a problem of plenty. With the I formation, there weren't enough backfield positions for Gilbert and two talented young fullbacks — junior-to-be Ted Koy and a youngster moving up from an undefeated freshman team, Steve Worster.

Royal had moved his newest assistant coach, Emory Bellard, from working with the defense during the 1967 season to backfield coach, and the two had talked about coming up with something new.

"I'd always messed with Split-T option football and always liked the concept, and of course, so had Darrell,"

Longtime friend and rival, USC coach John McKay, visits with Royal at a UT practice.

Bellard noted. "And so I got to messing with the triple option at the end of spring training. Because that's the only play in my opinion that's ever been devised in football that you can truly run effectively to the side where you've split somebody out and it's actually an asset rather than a detriment."

After running through a lot of chalk, pencil and paper, Bellard figured he finally had something early in the summer and showed it to Royal. They talked and talked about the triple-option concept with three backs lined up in formation opposite of the old Straight-T. Instead of the halfbacks up and the fullback a step back, Bellard had positioned the fullback

up behind the quarterback and the halfbacks a step back opposite each other.

"It fit right into everything I knew and learned from Coach Wilkinson," Royal said.

After much discussion and some further tinkering with blocking schemes and such, Royal decided they would put in the offense when the team reported back for two-a-days. That was a risk, but one Royal decided was worth taking. And it was greeted with enthusiasm by the squad — including Gilbert.

"When we put the Wishbone in, that was the highlight, the most fun part of my career," said Gilbert, who had amassed consecutive 1,000-yard rushing seasons out of the I-formation. "I was all in favor of it because I was the I-back and it was so easy to key. You just said here's one guy who is going to carry the ball and you try and stop him — no deception to it at all. You knew either Bill Bradley or I was going to have the ball.

"I was all in favor of it because we had so much talent on hand. I felt I wasn't going to carry the ball as much, but my average would go up. But what was so exciting was when we first ran it, we knew we were doing something no one else had done and was going to be impossible for the defense to pick up by scouting films of what we'd done the week before — because there was no week before when we first started."

But there was the shadow of the three previous seasons. Although the Longhorns followed their first national title by rolling to a 10-1 record and a final No. 5 ranking after upsetting the Crimson Tide, few could have predicted what was to follow.

"We had some injuries, but some of it wasn't that," Royal said. "We just weren't that good. We were kind of out of the running from me running around after our national championship.

"I was coach of the year and I felt kind of obligated to go to some things because of that. So I wasn't here on the weekends when we recruited. And I found out that you don't ever short Saturday during recruiting. You just decline any invitation you have on weekends.

"The staff worked just as hard, but I was traveling and was gone too much. They need the presence of the head coach. And it was passed around among recruits that, 'Well, the head coach of so-and-so came to see me. Did Texas' head coach come and see me?'

"So we didn't recruit well. But it didn't start showing up until they would have been juniors and seniors in 1966 and '67. You can't patch the problem if you don't have a strong junior and senior group. So we have three 6-and-4's (one 7-4 with a 19-0 win over Ole Miss in the

Royal had installed the Wishbone offense only during the preceding two-a-day practices but was poised to slide onto a track that would produce 30 consecutive victories, a piece of two more national titles and two of the greatest wins in Texas football history.

1966 Bluebonnet Bowl), and I knew we were in trouble. Then we really got busy and had a good group called the Worster Bunch, and you know what happened after that."

The decline actually started to show in 1965, though that season started out like many others. Texas rose to No. 1 the third week of the season and knocked off Oklahoma, 19-0, before the game with No. 3 Arkansas in The Hills. It was one of the best of the epic struggles between the two teams. Texas came from behind and scored late for a 24-20 lead. The Razorbacks scored later to win, 27-24. Subsequent injuries exposed a lack of depth. Texas then lost consecutive games to Rice and SMU.

"We had a pretty good team in 1965, but they just went to pot," Campbell offered. "I don't know what happened. But we were playing with players who just weren't as good as the ones in '62-63-64."

But for some reason recruiting got stronger. Before the Worster Bunch, Texas landed a class that included Koy, quarterback James Street, end Deryl Comer, linebacker Glenn Halsell and receiver Randy Peschel, among others. Worster was the top name in the 1967 class — which also had tackle Bobby Wuensch, linebacker Scott Henderson, end Bill Atessis and receiver Cotton Speyer.

"It's amazing when you think of it," Worster said. "Why would 13 blue-chippers decide to go to a school that just came off a 6-4 season?

"I came for a number of reasons — Coach Royal, the fact that Texas was such a first-class organization, just the whole system. Plus, I came rolling out of Bridge City, Tex., with swamps, mosquitoes, horrible humidity and terrible weather and I thought I was in heaven.

"They took me out to Lake Travis, I put my foot in the water and could see it! I said, damn, I didn't even realize they had places like this."

Worster said he had a small added push in the form of an unsigned letter from an Aggie, listing all the players

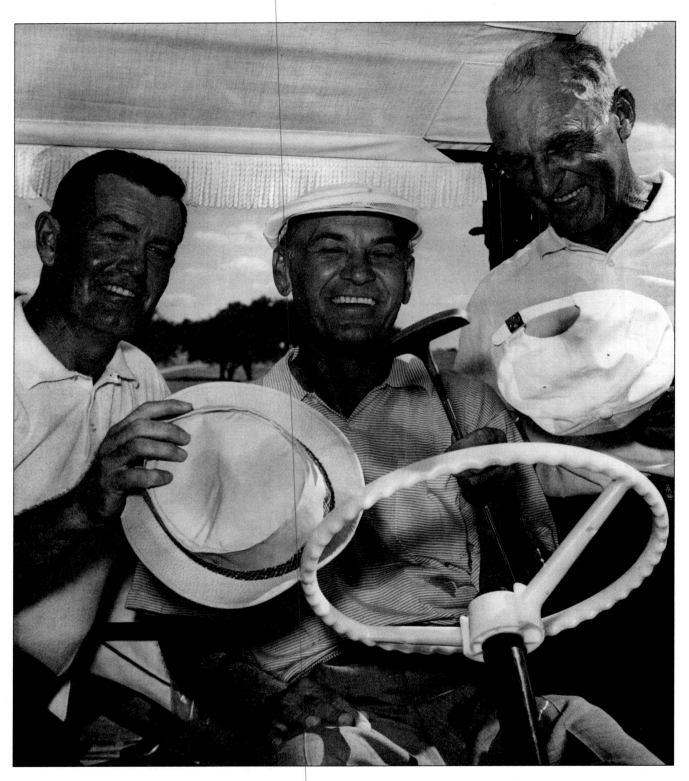

Royal and Rice coach Jess Neeley (right) receive a few golf tips from the legendary Ben Hogan.

with such-and-such high school credentials who were not playing prominent roles at Texas — an old recruiting ploy used against the Longhorns in the days before scholarship limits.

"Then," Worster remembered, "this letter said, 'Steve, all these boys are sitting on the bench at the University of Texas. How in the hell do you think you can play there?' And that pissed me off."

Worster and Koy had been the leading rushers in the spring game of 1968. And everyone could see they were going to mesh into the Wishbone. But after two games, it was obvious not everything was yet shifting smoothly. Two things changed that. First, after the Houston and Tech games, Worster was moved a step back off the quarterback's rear end to give him better vision of what was unfolding ahead and to give the two more maneuvering room. And James Street took over for Bradley at quarterback.

"Bill Bradley was the best all-around athlete we had," Royal said. "But he could not operate under the restrictions and discipline required as the quarterback. He was the kind of guy you need to put out there and just let play.

"There's no telling how many interceptions he would have had if we'd played him in the secondary all those years. Of course he went on to a great pro career playing defense (with the Philadelphia Eagles), but he would have been everybody's all-American in college. And it was a tough move. But we had to make it, because we couldn't have the controversy of Bradley and Street at the same position."

There was no controversy from the first moment that Bradley came out for drills on the Monday before the Oklahoma State game — after Street had come in for him and moved the team smartly the Saturday before against Tech. Bradley threw some, worked at corner some and then lined up with the receivers to run pass patterns.

"I give so much credit to Bill the way he handled things," Street said. "We worked out in sweats on Monday. We were running patterns over the middle, and he had untied his sweatpants to where they would fall down while he was running his pattern. That broke everybody up. And it broke the ice because everyone knew that Bill wasn't mad, that nobody's feelings were hurt.

"Before the (Oklahoma State) game, Bradley got up in front of the team and told them that The Rat — he called me The Rat — was going to take us to victory and we just needed to give him some support."

The Rat did take them to victory — nine of them in 1968 beginning with a 31-3 swamping of Oklahoma State and 11 more the next season, including the storied Big Shootout victory over Arkansas and the historic win over Notre Dame in the 1970 Cotton Bowl.

But some forget who did just what. Street said he was recently waiting in line at an ice cream parlor in Austin when a stranger approached, introduced himself and talked about how many memories he had given him while he was in school at Texas in the late 1960's. He then asked if he could bring his family in to meet him.

Street graciously said yes. The guy brought in his troops, made introductions all around and said, "This is the greatest quarterback in Texas history — Bill Bradley."

A friend who was with Street turned around to hide his laughter. Street struggled to keep a straight face.

"I didn't want to embarrass the guy in front of his family, so I just thanked him for his compliments. Later that summer I saw Bradley and told him I still couldn't beat him out in some people's minds."

But after the Oklahoma State game, it was clear that Street was here to stay. Which requires the re-telling of a key moment in Royal's recruitment of Street. The two were sitting in the press box during Street's visit the fall of his senior year watching the freshman team play the Aggie fish. Bradley was the quarterback.

"Bill did everything," Street said. "He ran, he passed, he intercepted. He looked great.

"So Coach Royal mentioned that he imagined everyone else was throwing Bill up to me and he said that if I started running away from competition, I would never know whether or not I could play with the best. He just kind of threw that out there and I had the feeling that he didn't care if I liked it or not — if I responded to that, good. If I didn't, that would be good, too."

Street thought about Royal's comments for two weeks. Then he committed to Texas.

And now, two years later as Street took over for Bradley, it began to dawn on everyone that he and this new formation were made for each other and that something special was on the horizon.

"James was wound like a nine-day clock," Bellard said. "He was made for the Wishbone. I knew what we had and that if we did it right we were going to be good.

"I think in Oklahoma State we beat a football team that was not as good as we were. The one I felt good about was when we beat Oklahoma (26-20) the following week. I think at that point we started doing things the way they were supposed to be done and everything started to fall into place. We had a good win there. We moved the ball very, very good. And from then on, we just got stronger, stronger, stronger and stronger."

And the scores began to mount as teams scrambled for defensive schemes to match this new weapon. Ranked No. 17, Texas followed the Oklahoma victory by disposing of No. 9 Arkansas, 39-29. Then followed victories over Rice (38-14), SMU (38-7), Baylor (47-26), TCU (47-21) and Texas A&M (35-14) and the first Southwest Conference title since 1963 — the first of five in a row.

As lopsided as those scores were, Gilbert said they could have been worse.

"Coach Royal never believed in individual or team records," he noted. "A lot of those games were over by halftime and Coach Royal would clear the bench. He tried to be generous during those next years.

"Darrell and Emory were both super putting in those plays and it was so much fun seeing them develop in practice because we were doing things that no one else in football was doing. And at one time, we all started feeling like we were bullet-proof.

"By the end of the season, we felt that absolutely no one could hang with us. Not only did we have a good group of athletes, we had this incredible offense and our defense was coming around like gang-busters."

The Longhorns broke six Southwest Conference rushing records — including most yards gained (4,476), most yards rushing (3,315) and the highest scoring average in SWC history (38 points).

Gilbert was a consensus all-American and with 1,132 yards became the first player in NCAA history to have three consecutive thousand-yard seasons. Worster (with 806 yards) and Koy (601) combined for more than 1,400 yards.

Texas capped the season by ripping No. 8 Tennessee in the Cotton Bowl, 36-13, after which the Longhorns rose to No. 3 as The Associated Press was now doing a vote after the bowl games.

"That's the way you want to go out," Gilbert said. "There were no problems on the team, everyone had a great year and they kept it on a roll."

Better things were to come on the football field, where it was now apparent that Darrell Royal would end his career wearing the Orange and White.

It had always been assumed that Oklahoma would make a run at Royal when Bud Wilkinson stepped down, as he did to run for the Senate in early 1964. Coincidentally, Texas officials had decided at a meeting in December before the Cotton Bowl victory over Navy to give Royal a raise (to $24,000) and the rank of full professor tied to his athletic directorship post and university tenure. They announced it in February as Wilkinson was strong-arming longtime aide Gomer Jones into becoming his successor.

But Jones couldn't hack it. Oklahoma was 6-4-1 in his first season, including a loss to Florida State in the Gator Bowl after he had to drop four players from his squad who had already signed pro contracts. The Sooners won only three games in 1965 and lost to Oklahoma State for the first time in 20 years. Jones was forced out and the rumors about Royal spread like wildfire. They were fanned by an AP report on Sunday, December 12, that the OU athletic council had unanimously recommended Royal's hiring.

OU President Dr. George Cross was quoted as saying, "I have talked to Mr. Royal and he is interested. We would not make the offer except with the expectation that he would accept."

But the next day, Cross backtracked. "I want to assure the Texas public," he told The Dallas Times Herald, "that we are not sure at all if (Royal) would accept."

There was a reason. Out of courtesy, Royal did talk with Oklahoma officials, but did not owe them the discourtesy of publicly down-playing his interest. The OU council's bold statement was later viewed as a grandstand play to satisfy their fans that they had made the effort to lure Royal, before hiring Jim McKenzie.

Royal listens while Texas Governor Allen Shivers explains the Wishbone-T to Joe Namath.

Royal says he never considered a concrete offer. On that Monday, he announced he was staying at Texas.

"I never listened to the offer because I didn't want Texas to feel like they had to match it," Royal said. "And what if it had been the right kind of offer? Then I've got to decide, do I want to go or do I want to stay? I felt that if I talked to them (seriously), then I would have to have my mind made up that I would take the job with the right kind of offer.

"I love Oklahoma. But even though Gomer Jones did an in-betweener, I wasn't following Wilkinson. I felt like up there everybody still remembered my playing days and something about that familiarity just didn't hold with

me. When I came to Texas, I was in a new setting. They didn't know me as a player, but as a football coach and I felt that was valuable to me. And I was already established at Texas and my family was here."

Royal has never second-guessed his decision.

"Everything worked out," he said. "My gut feeling (that again) turned out to be right. That would not have been a good move for me. I don't know what might have happened to me up there. But I know what happened to me down here."

Royal had yet to face two more of his leanest years at Texas. But as 1968 became 1969, he was poised for one of the greatest runs of his, or any other coach's, career.

CHAPTER ELEVEN

The Big Shootout

With a President and a National TV Audience Watching, Texas and Arkansas Battled in The Game of the Century

His head swimming, perhaps somewhat stunned by the message he was taking back into the Texas huddle, James Street took four or five steps out onto the field. But then he stopped and retreated a few steps toward Darrell Royal on the sideline.

"I wasn't questioning the play," Street said. "I just wanted to be sure. All I said was, 'Right 53 veer pass, which means we're going to set Cotton Speyer — our best receiver — to the wide side of the field and we're gonna run the throwback pattern deep to the tight end. Are you sure that's the call you want?'

"Coach Royal looked me right in the eye and said, 'Damn right I'm sure!'"

In a similar story with a naval setting, Royal might have replied, "Damn the torpedoes. Full speed ahead." But behind his short and definitive reply to Street was the knowledge, savvy and the intuition of a lifetime capsuled into what became the definitive moment of Royal's coaching career.

Some six weeks later between semesters, Street felt the need to get away from it all. For Street, getting away meant Las Vegas. He checked into the Las Vegas Hilton that day in January 1970 and the hotel manager, who hap-

pened to be nearby and was a college football fan, introduced himself and asked it there was anything he could do for him during his stay. Street told him, yeah, he would like to meet Elvis Presley, who was appearing in the ballroom at the hotel.

The manager said, no problem. Come to the show the next night and Colonel Tom Parker, Elvis' manager, would come get him afterward and take him backstage. Things worked out just so, but Street was in for something of a surprise.

"Bill Medley, one of the Righteous Brothers, comes back," Street recounted. "And it turns out that both had watched the Arkansas game on television. So there I am in the same room with my hero (Elvis), and here's Elvis and one of the Righteous Brothers arguing about the Texas-Arkansas game.

"Medley says it was a stupid call and that Arkansas should have won. Elvis disagreed and says Texas rightfully won. I couldn't believe it. But that whole year was incredible."

Indeed, college football's 100th anniversary could have had no more fitting climax than that unforgettable matchup between the two undefeated teams from Texas and Arkansas who were ranked 1-2 in the nation, playing before a truly national television audience estimated at more than 50 million and such in-stadium dignitaries as President Richard M. Nixon and evangelist Billy Graham.

Randy Peschel caught the pass that set up the game-winning touchdown for the Longhorns.

Texas had won 18 consecutive games. Arkansas was unbeaten through 15.

"What a game," recalled Chris Schenkel, ABC's top announcer of the day who described the game to millions from the press box, along with color analyst Bud Wilkinson.

"You've got everything surrounding the game and you've got two of the best buddies that ever were, Darrell Royal and Frank Broyles, going head to head. Plus the President, senators, congressmen. My goodness."

Even Royal had to concede that 1969, the Big Shootout and the climatic victory over Notre Dame in the Cotton Bowl that clinched his fourth national championship was a script with all the twists and turns of fiction.

"With all the things that happened, it was quite a year," he said. "And you couldn't have set a stage better than the one that was set for the Arkansas game."

Moved to a regular-season ending date of Dec. 7 at the original suggestion of ABC publicist Beano Cook, it was for many, The Game of the Century.

Many young Americans had other things on their minds as the first week of December dawned. On Monday night, the initial lottery drawing for the military draft was held and the specter of the growingly unpopular Viet Nam war divided the country.

"My (draft) number was 264," Randy Peschel recalled. "But I didn't even watch the show on television. My girlfriend called to tell me. The excitement about the game was at an intense level. I don't remember doing much in school. I always went to class, but I don't remember anything that went on."

Royal and requested players conducted endless interviews with the press.

"But we had our workouts, we didn't let anything interfere with that," noted Royal, who tried to prepare his team for playing in Razorback Stadium in Fayetteville.

"Coach Royal kept trying to tell us about playing up there, but I couldn't figure out why," Street said. "I didn't figure it was any different than playing in Little Rock, Dallas or anywhere else. I was wrong."

After what players would describe as an awe-inspiring Thursday night pep rally in Memorial Stadium that drew an estimated 35,000, the Longhorns arrived in Fayetteville on Friday. They held a short workout in the stadium and then got out of town, on down the road to a hotel in Rogers, some 30 miles away. Broyles likewise hustled his team out of town, which was already a madhouse by Friday afternoon. Easy Rider was playing at a local theater. A sign in front of a church read, "Pigs Broyles Steers. Services Sunday."

On a later observation of the same church sign, Royal observed wryly, "I had hoped God would be neutral."

But the coach left little to chance. On the bus from Rogers to Razorback Stadium, he called his quarterback up to sit beside him.

"Coach Royal had never done that before," Street said. "He explained to me that if we got into a situation where we were going to have to go for two, this was the play we were going to run and to go ahead and take it to the outside option."

For not the last time that day, Street wondered what Royal could be thinking.

"I had seen the films of Arkansas playing Baylor a couple of weeks before and Baylor had run all over them (though the Bears lost, 35-19). I didn't think we were going to kill 'em, but I didn't think we were going to get into a situation where we would need to go for two."

Intuition? Or perhaps Royal was thinking back to a 14-13 loss to the Hogs in 1964 when a late try for two points failed, costing Texas a possible second consecutive national title. Royal never regretted that earlier decision, which was in keeping with his competitive drive for nothing less but victory, be it on the football field or in a game of chess. He only regrets that his instructions on the specific play called were not specific enough.

"Well you know, sometimes you've just got to anticipate," Royal said. "I knew with all the fanfare, we had to be ready if the situation came up."

Royal had visited early in the week with defensive coordinator Mike Campbell and asked him what play gave him the most problem defending a goal-line situation. Campbell replied the counter-option. So that's the play Royal outlined for Street in a more-or-less peaceful setting on the way to the stadium.

As usual, Royal was several moves ahead of mere mortals — though the Arkansas defense was a step ahead from the beginning of that game. And the Razorbacks' offense was doing some damage of its own behind quarterback Bill

Montgomery. The Hogs led, 14-0, after Chuck Dicus — who caught nine passes for 146 yards — hauled in a 29-yard scoring reception less than six minutes into the second half.

Texas' offense, meanwhile, had been all but stymied by Arkansas' defensive play, and Royal could no doubt hear experts all over the country intoning how the Wishbone was not a come-from-behind offense.

"They had us confused with the defense they were playing," Royal admitted. "They were smart. They outfoxed us. After that, we changed our blocking patterns. They tried to play us the same way the next year and we scored on our first three possessions (and won, 42-7)."

But on that cold, foggy afternoon in Fayetteville, the Longhorns, who turned the ball over three times, were trailing, 14-0, and had shown little life until Street turned a busted play into a 42-yard touchdown run on the first play of the fourth quarter.

"It's easy to say now, but I never thought we were go-ing to get beat," Street said. "I was still going into the huddle and telling everyone that everything was going to be OK, all we've got to do is execute. But about that time (center) Bob McKay said, 'Hey, it's not OK. It's time. We've got to do something.'

"But if you ask the players, I don't think any of them thought we were going to lose. And Coach Royal never panicked. I felt totally confident that he would figure out some way for us to win the ball game."

Street's touchdown run was a called pass.

"I was trying to hit Peschel across the middle, but McKay actually missed his block and they kept driving me to the left on the weak side. The linebacker was between me and Randy, so I had no choice but to take off running. I just kind of squeezed though there, the safety slipped and I slipped right on in behind him."

Here, Royal's visit with Street on the bus paid dividends. After the touchdown, he waved Street back in-

President Richard Nixon traveled to Fayetteville to award the winner a national championship trophy.

to the game. Street knew what he was thinking.

"By him having already given me the play, I was totally prepared and I could get the guys together in the huddle and explain it without there being any confusion over what we were going to do," Street said.

"Coach Royal wasn't one of those rah-rah guys, he wasn't putting any worms in his mouth or anything like that to get you ready. No gimmicks to it. It was just like we're going to go out there and beat these guys because we're prepared to do what we have to do and we're going to do it. That's what he expected."

After the touchdown, Street took the counter option outside and slipped into the end zone to cut the deficit to 14-8. And then came another telling turn of events.

Montgomery moved the Razorbacks methodically downfield to a third and goal at the UT 7. Rather than lay up for a field goal that would have forced Texas to score at least twice to win, Arkansas called a pass. Montgomery threw behind Dicus on an out pattern. Danny Lester leaped high to intercept the pass, rather than bat it away, and raced to the UT 20.

"You have the decisions to make and you have to live with the outcome," Frank Broyles said afterward. "It was a safe pattern to run — normally."

Royal shook his head at the memory. "If Danny Lester doesn't intercept that pass ..."

Texas then mounted a drive, but soon suffered its fourth turnover on a fumble at the Arkansas 39. The Longhorn defense forced a punt. But Texas gained only seven yards on three ensuing running plays.

And then, it was fourth and three at the Texas 42 with 4:47 to play. Texas called time and Street went to the sideline where Royal was talking to Emory Bellard in the press box upstairs.

Leon Manley was one of the three coaches up there.

"Emory is talking to Darrell and all of the sudden he says, " 'Pass?' And I say, 'Pass?'"

Royal was not a the mood for a discussion, or a debate.

"I pulled my headset off and stopped talking to the press box. It was just James and me," Royal said. "Man,

Jim Bertelsen dives across the goal line to put the Longhorns on top, 15-14.

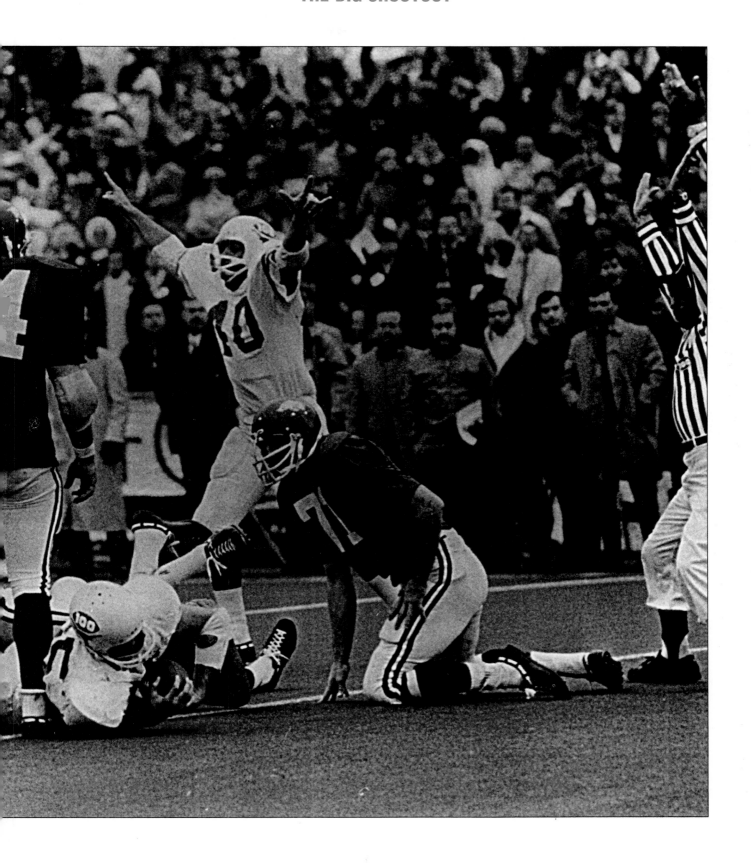

they were going nuts up there in the booth.”

Street also was in the process of giving birth to a small feline.

“I thought, ‘Where in the hell did he come up with that?’ We hadn’t even talked about using that play. It wasn’t in our short-yardage plays, it wasn’t in our goal-line plays.”

But Royal remembered that Peschel had told him at halftime that most of the time the Arkansas secondary was committing early to stopping the run, and that if needed, he might be able to go deep on them.

Apparently, no one else was aware.

“I wanted to run a formation to the wide side of the field, and so did Coach Bellard, because all day Arkansas had over-shifted to the wide side,” Street said. “I told Coach Royal I figured we could run the counter-option and I could dive in there and make three yards or pitch and make more than that.

“But then Coach Royal took his headset off. And here is where the difference in being a real good coach and a great coach comes — the ability to make the call without ever thinking about the repercussions if it didn’t work or what anyone was going to think or say. He knew the significance of the play as far that game and history was concerned. But he didn’t think a thing about it.”

Damn right he was sure.

And so after his brief re-consultation, Street hustled out to the huddle to break the news.

Randy Peschel well remembers the moment.

“James came back into the huddle and he said, ‘Peschel, don’t look at me.’ And I’m wondering what in the world is all this about? Then he looks directly at Cotton and said, ‘We’re going to run Right 53 veer pass.’ ”

Fullback Steve Worster, anticipating he might get the ball, was just as stunned as the rest of the players.

“Chins dropped. Total disbelief,” said Worster, who gouged out a tough 94 yards on 25 carries that day. “But I was fascinated by the call. I mean it was such a big play. The whole game revolved around that play. I couldn’t believe that we were throwing the ball, but at the same time we weren’t doing worth a damn on the ground, so why not?”

The ever-aware Street knew what he was doing when he called the play looking right at Cotton Speyer.

“The way we had our huddle set up,” Street explained, “Cotton was right in front of me beside the center. All day

Arkansas was looking into our huddle, so I pointed my finger right at Cotton but said, ‘I’m talking to you, Randy, and ya’ll are not going to believe this play; but it’s going to work.’ ”

Since the play was not in the Arkansas game package, Street explained in detail what was to happen so there would be no confusion. And while gesturing to Speyer, he quickly told Peschel that if he saw he couldn’t shake loose deep, to make sure he was at least three yards downfield and come back or run an out pattern and he would just dump the ball to him for the first down.

But as Street called, “Ready, break!” he was hit by a minor panic.

“My fear was what if just about the time I released the ball Peschel had stopped and started back toward me? How was I going to explain that to Coach Royal?”

Fortunately for Street, he never had to.

“I took an inside release. And I can remember very vividly making the commitment to go for it instead of cutting it off and just trying to get the first down,” said Peschel, who also suffered a small tremor when he saw the football in the air.

“I remember thinking that I was never going to catch it because I thought it was going to be over my head. I wasn’t very fleet afoot. I had them fooled for awhile, but they caught up to me.”

Defensive backs Jerry Moore and Dennis Berner converged rapidly.

“I knew it was on target when I threw the ball,” Street said. “As Bobby Layne used to say, it’s like shooting a shotgun. You look at the bird and shoot. But I didn’t know if I’d thrown it where someone other than Randy was going to catch it.”

Peschel didn’t know either until he clutched the ball to his chest and fell to the soggy turf at the Arkansas 13.

“I remember seeing the ball come down and I see two pairs of hands stretched out,” Peschel said. “And the ball floats over their fingers by six inches and right into my hands.”

As Peschel made the catch, Texas fans all across America went berserk. So did Worster, who stayed in to block.

“I just went bananas,” he said. “It was like a dream. But we had such total trust in our coaches, we never doubted anything they said. We would run through fire and hell for them. So you were kind of astonished at first

The Longhorns posted an 11-0-0 record in 1969 and were named national champions.

and then you just kind of said, well … and went on."

Street was buried shortly after his release by nose guard Terry Don Phillips, a former Longview teammate.

"I saw the referee signal 'catch' and point our way — and I still get chills thinking about it," Street said. "I said to Terry Don, 'Come on, bubba. We're way down here now.' I was excited, but I knew the work wasn't over with."

Neither were the quirks of fate that played so well throughout Royal's life. On the next play, halfback Jim Bertelsen couldn't throw his assigned block on the defensive lineman — so he passed him up and cut down the linebacker, which sprung Ted Koy for an 11-yard gain. After looking at the film, the offensive staff changed the halfback's assignment to the linebacker against that defensive set.

Bertelsen scored on the next play and Happy Feller kicked the critical point-after with 3:58 to play. Plenty of time for Montgomey and his pals to mount another scor-

ing drive, reminiscent of the late march in 1965 that had sent the top-ranked Longhorns spinning into three sub-par seasons.

But Tom Campbell — who would also save the 21-17 victory over Notre Dame in the Cotton Bowl with an interception — stepped in front of John Rees to steal a Montgomery pass at the Texas 21 with 1:13 to play.

It was over.

Street is touched today by a moment of pathos from the immediate bedlam of the game's final gun.

"Just a minute in time," he said. "I was totally worn out, exhausted and inside wanting to bust out with total exhilaration. But I remember seeing these two little girls, crying and running up to Coach Broyles. I found out later they were his twin daughters. I told him years later that that was the first time I realized that for every winner in a game, there had to be a loser."

CHAPTER TWELVE

Down the Stretch

Texas' Greatest College Football Coach Marches to Gridiron Glory in the 1970's and Retirement

Steve Worster was in Austin on business not long after he graduated from the University of Texas when, not on impulse, but out of a deep-seated need, he called Darrell Royal and said he needed to talk.

"God, I needed help," Worster said. "And Coach Royal was the first person I thought of because I knew he would give me a good, solid answer and steer me in the direction I needed to go. He has a way of tuning in to you and what he tells you is very believable. No bullshit."

Worster was wrestling with both fame and infamy. He was one of the major players and most recognizable figures on the powerful 1969 and 1970 teams that stormed out of the Big Shootout victory over Arkansas to the widely acclaimed victory over Notre Dame in the 1970 Cotton Bowl and beyond. The victory string eventually reached 30 games, before Notre Dame ended it — as it had clipped Oklahoma's 47-game streak in 1956 — in a New Year's Day 1971 rematch so succinctly capsulized in a lead written by Walter Robertson, then sports editor of The Dallas Morning News:

"Time marched on into another new year Friday, but without a traveling companion which had been almost as certain for nearly three long years."

Not only fame but a degree of infamy hounded Worster. Playing that day with painful rib and knee injuries that had severely limited his workout time for the last five weeks of the season, the all-American fullback fumbled three times among the six turnovers suffered by the Texas offense and gained only 45 yards on 16 carries.

It had been Royal who found him in a corner of the Cotton Bowl dressing room and told him to get out and face the music.

"I had my head so far gone I couldn't see daylight," Worster said. "He said, "You were out there when we were kicking everyone's fanny the last 30 games, you're going to be out there when we lose one.' I got out there and took the grief."

Though playing on teams that won 30 of 33 games in three seasons had been the ride of his life, Worster was now ready to get off. He didn't know how.

"It had gotten to the point where I was embarrassed to introduce myself, to even say who I was anymore," Worster recalled. "I'd just say I was Steve and not even tell people my last name until someone asked. Then they'd go, 'Oh, yeah!' and make a big deal out of it. And that would turn out even worse because they would think I was setting them up. It seemed like I was just running in circles."

Royal and Worster met at one of Royal's favorite East Austin eating establishments, where Worster found the peace he was seeking.

"He said that I had played hard and worked my ass off for every accolade. That nothing had been given to me that I didn't work for and didn't deserve and it was there to be appreciated. And if that didn't fly with people, fine. Don't expect it to. That I had earned my place.

"What he told me just made my life so much easier after that. I guess I just needed my mentor, my main man to tell me that."

Royal was soon to face his own demons of one sort or another as he came into his third decade as the head coach at the University of Texas.

Many triumphs were yet to come. Royal's teams would win four more Southwest Conference championships. The 1972 team finished No. 3 nationally and defeated Alabama in the Cotton Bowl. The '75 Longhorns —

Royal's next-to-last team — ranked No. 6 at season's end after knocking off Colorado in the Bluebonnet Bowl.

But on the field, Royal's mastery of Oklahoma was at an end. Beginning with a 47-28 loss in 1971, Texas would not again taste victory under Royal in the storied series in which he played such a major role as both player and coach. The final 6-6 tie with the Sooners in 1976 — the Spy Game — he would later rank as his most bitter "defeat."

Off the field, his disenchantment with the game that had been so much a part of his life was growing. As he said publicly, he was angered by the deceit he now found in recruiting and by the growing cheating involved.

"I still enjoyed the games," Royal said. "I enjoyed the coaching. I enjoyed the competition. I still enjoyed getting immersed in a game plan. But (because of) the deceitfulness, the cheating ... I got so I didn't like to recruit."

There were still those who dealt from an honest deck.

"There were a lot of cases where things were still straight-arrow," he said. "But it got so that you didn't know how truthful the feedback and response you were getting from either the family or the prospect was.

"Prospects would do themselves and the schools a favor if they would make a decision about what they want to do instead of leading you on and hoping you are going to give them something extra right up to signing day. Just tell you one way or the other."

Royal visits with his longtime rival, Arkansas coach Frank Broyles, who he defeated, 29-12, in his final game in 1976.

Also, Royal came under personal attack. He weathered a storm of controversy stirred by a book, *Meat on the Hoof*, written in the late 1960's by a former squadman, an account with more than one fabrication and a skewed view that the author said was as much an indictment of a system as of a particular coach. But Royal was portrayed as uncaring, a brutal and aloof taskmaster.

That's not the person Doug English remembers.

"Coach Royal is man who stands for certain principles," said English, an all-American defensive tackle in 1974 who is now an Austin wholesaler of computer components and still close to his former coach.

"He was always there for the players who worked hard, who spent a little extra time running or in the weight room. Who fulfilled their obligations to the school in terms of making their grades, who were a part of the program that he laid down. You could either participate or not.

"Some guys whined about how Coach Royal never paid any attention to them. That Coach Royal wouldn't speak to them. That Coach Royal didn't do this or that. Well, those are the same guys who decided they'd rather be the best beer-chugger in their fraternity, or a bartender or the next Jimmie Hendrix — and I'm dating myself now.

"But those guys never fulfilled their commitment to the coach or to the rest of us to put in the extra effort to make themselves better day after day, week after week. Coach Royal's attitude was that if you'd like to participate, then you have a good friend. If not, I'll be nice to you but I have too many other people to whom I have obligations. You be honest and be a man and I'll be there for you.

"He was that way then and he's that way now," English said.

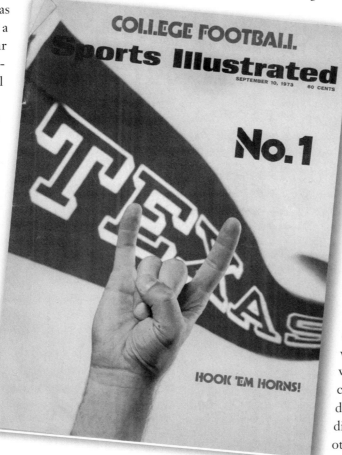

But as tough as the illegal recruiting problems were to weather for Royal, they were nothing compared to the loss of his daughter, Marian, in a traffic accident in March 1972 — later compounded by an accident in the same vicinity that took David in the same month nine years later.

"That's something you never get over," said Royal, who naturally is reluctant to talk about the losses. "Time helps with the pain, but you never get over it."

"It's just something you really don't talk to anyone else about unless they have experienced it," Edith said. "There were times when I thought we wouldn't make it — mainly because of the different ways we dealt with our grief — but we did and life's been pretty good other than those times."

As the 1970's marched on, however, Royal became increasingly disenchanted with certain aspects of his profession. On the drive back from the 1974 loss to Baylor — the Miracle on the Brazos — Campbell said Royal told him he didn't know how much longer he would coach.

Leon Manley said Royal gave him similar vibes when he went to him after the 1974 season and told him he was considering going with Fred Akers to Wyoming.

"I told him Fred had offered me more money to be his line coach, but that Wyoming wasn't Texas," Manley recalled. "And he told me then he might coach two more weeks, a year or two more years. That he just didn't know. I was surprised. I thought he was telling me something then."

By late October 1976, Royal made up his mind that this would be his last season.

"It was before the Texas Tech game (October 30) that I got the idea that would be his last season," Edith said. "He said, 'I'm not enjoying the winning and the losses are just devastating.' That was the first time he had said something like that. I think he decided after that game that it was time."

The night of December 4, 1976, will be remembered by many as the day the music died in the Southwest Conference. Certainly an era in college football passed on that mist-shrouded night in Memorial Stadium. Royal and longtime friend and foe Frank Broyles both coached their last games. Texas won, 29-12, to run an injury-plagued season's record to 5-5-1 and preserve Royal's string of never having a losing season as a head coach.

When asked his reaction to his 100th victory as a head coach (in 1966), Royal replied it felt no different than the first, but that he would like to win his last.

"I didn't think it was important to have a big final season, but to win the last one to me personally was a big deal."

Royal and Broyles met at midfield after the final gun, where they embraced among the swirl of players and swarm of media.

"I love you," Royal said.

"I love you, too," Broyles replied.

Each had known weeks before that the other would retire, but each reached the same decision independently.

Former quarterback Ted Constanzo remembers that night vividly.

"You know, you have the feeling that life goes on forever, but of course it doesn't," Constanzo said. "That night is a snapshot in history. And to have been a part of that, words can't really express."

Some things that influenced his decision to leave his life's profession, Royal even now will not discuss in total. That includes the stinging disappointment when his wish was not honored that Mike Campbell succeed him and the infighting that surrounded his final years — when some closely connected with the university were critical of among other things, Royal's open association with his guitar-picker friends.

"I'm not going to talk about any of that political stuff that went on because some of the people involved are not around to offer their opinions," Royal stated.

Others will talk, including English.

"Suddenly, Darrell looks up and a game that he's worked his whole life in — a game of who works the hardest and prepares the best wins — has become a game where the ones who cheat the best, the ones who spy the best, who lie the best are all gaining footholds.

"Now there's more money in the game. You've got schools buying players. And a lot of really nasty things are being done by people with no character — and that includes coaches, players, alumni and administrators. And Coach Royal said that's not me — he's not going to sit and listen to an 18-year-old kid tell him that he's got to buy him a new pickup truck to come to the University of Texas.

"So I think his decision to retire at 52 years old was consistent with a man who has certain beliefs and prin-

THE FIRST COUPLE OF COLLEGE FOOTBALL:
Darrell and Edith Royal, in 1975.

Royal and Joe Paterno at a Cotton Bowl press conference prior to their New Year's game in 1972.

ciples and that's it. They ain't gonna change. You can either chose to participate or carry your show somewhere else. And that's what he did."

Late on the night of his retirement at his final, traditional post-game gathering with the press in room 2001 at the since-demolished Villa Capri, Royal noted, "You've got to remember that I've been a head coach 24 years. I've just used up a lot of ammunition in that time. I wanted to get out before I was spent.

"I'm not tired of coaching, but I wanted to get out before I got tired of it. I always wanted to leave somebody's house when they wanted me to stay a little longer. It's a good idea to leave a little ham on the bone."

Some thought that Royal should have retired when he was on top. Not so, he said.

"I felt like it was an ideal time, because we had some great material there. I thought that was a good time to quit because, among others, Earl Campbell was coming

back, and he was a load right there."

Perhaps apropos is reference to a poem that Royal used to recite, one given him once by a pastor friend to help him overcome an early fear of public speaking. It is a poem that Royal would call and recite over the phone to Bill Alexander until he could overcome a sing-song delivery and simply tell the story.

The guts of the poem deals with the reply of an old man in response to a question as to why he would labor to build a bridge across a river that he had already crossed.

And the builder raised his old gray head:
"Good friend, on the path that I have come," he said,
"There followeth after me today
A youth whose feet will pass this way.
This stream, which has been naught to me,
To that fair-haired boy may a pitfall be;
He, too, must cross in the twilight dim —
Good friend, I am building this bridge for him."

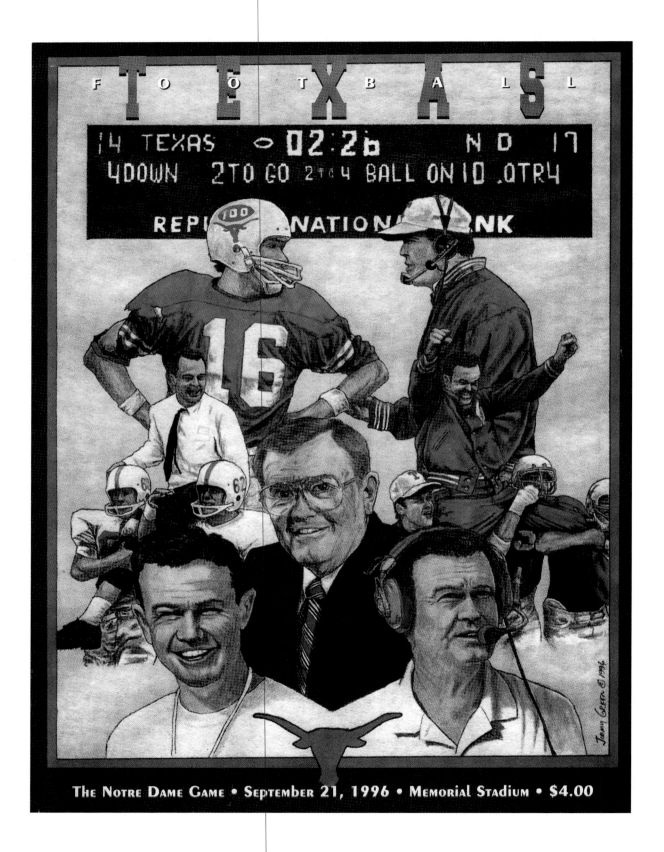

TEXAS FOOTBALL

14 TEXAS 0 02:26 ND 17
4 DOWN 2 TO GO 2 TO 4 BALL ON 10 .QTR 4

REPUBLIC NATIONAL BANK

The Notre Dame Game • September 21, 1996 • Memorial Stadium • $4.00

CHAPTER THIRTEEN

Beyond the Whistle

After a Storied Career, Royal Begins to Enjoy the Rewards of 20 Years on the Longhorns Sideline

Edith Royal recently came home one midday to find Darrell at the kitchen table wolfing down a fast-food hamburger, something he usually doesn't eat. But that day he had been to take a physical examination, run another errand and had returned home where he was in the middle of planning the Ben Willie Darrell golf tournament and had no time for a proper meal.

"I just stood there looking at him gobbling that thing down," Edith said. "He was back in his old firehouse mode, thinking about the next thing he had to do. I finally said, 'Darrell, you don't have to make a kickoff, so slow down.' He had no idea he was gobbling that burger down. Darrell is usually pretty calm these days, but he can get back into that mode sometimes without even realizing it."

In the early years of Royal's retirement, Edith's adjustment may have been more difficult.

"I think it was easier for him than me. When he retired, I thought it was temporary. That surely he was going to do something else. I kept trying to find him another job for 10 years and so did his friends.

"But things have worked out so well and I'm so glad Darrell did it like he did," she said. "He has been able to really enjoy the last years of his life. I have seen so many people wait until they are 70 to retire and they died two years later. But Darrell has really enjoyed his time. He's happy and he's been useful. I think he's at peace."

Problems with arthritis have raised Royal's golf handicap — to around eight or nine. He is now extremely interested in politics and says he seldom reads the sports section. But he plays golf almost daily with friends or former players, who frequently call to visit, stir up a game or invite the Royals to supper.

"That's one of the true rewards of staying in one place for 40 years," Royal said. "You still have the bond between former players and their coach, but in the years afterward you get to become friends. I see a lot of former players from time to time and it's great to see how successful most of them have become. I can't stay in close contact with every one of them, but the ones who choose to stay in contact, I love it."

Royal is equally in close contact with his assortment of guitar-pickers, song-writers and performers — most of whom will quickly tell you they like Coach Royal but they love Edith. And she remembers when they formed the close association with the country and western entertainment segment during their early years in Austin.

"I believe it was Buck Owens that Darrell first invited to a game," she said. "It was at the Cotton Bowl, but I don't remember if it was an Oklahoma game or the Cotton Bowl game.

"Darrell told me that he had invited Buck to sit with me in the press box. And I was scared to death that he was going to show up in a rhinestone suit, because that's all I'd ever seen him in. But he showed up in jeans and a T-shirt just like anyone else. Buck and I are still friends."

Royal has long been a music lover, including the big bands. But his real fascination is with songwriters.

"I really admire them," he said. "They've got two and a-half minutes to tell their story and they can't hem-haw and beat around the bush, they've got to get to it.

"I've stolen and copied ways of expressing myself from songwriters. Once I understood their role, I always felt that the press didn't want a long, drawn-out explanation. They wanted something they could write. And they couldn't write a book."

The "Royalisms," as they came to be known, are

Royal and five of his favorite golf buddies: (left to right) Willie Nelson, Andy Williams, Bob Hope, Robert Sakowitz and Doug Sanders in 1988.

legend. The most famous, perhaps, came in 1965 after consecutive losses to Rice and SMU. Royal was asked if he planned any changes.

"My confidence isn't shaken about our methods of doing things," he said. "There's an old saying. 'You dance with who brung ya.' We'll keep on doing the things that have worked so well for us through the years."

There was of course the "Luck is when preparation meets opportunity" observation that so many of his former players took to heart in their business careers. A few others:

The post-script to the luck observation: "Breaks even out. The sun don't shine on the same dog's rear end every day."

On poor coverage of a punt: "You'd have thought we'd be on it like a hen on a june bug. Punt returns can kill you faster than a minnow can swim a dipper."

On reality: "Old ugly is better than old nothin'."

On state of mind: "You've got to think lucky. If you fall into a mudhole, check your back pocket — you might have caught a fish."

On losing a game in the last minute: "It was like having a big ol' lollipop in your mouth and the first thing you know, all you have is the stick."

On the kind of player he liked to recruit: "Give me a guy with his jaw stuck out, his shirt sleeves rolled up and who swaggers when he walks. I know it's Harry High School, but if I have to make a choice I'll take the cocky, over-confident, conceited kid over the one who has so much humility he can't look you in the eye."

On life: "If everything had already been done, there would be nothing left for young people to accomplish. There are always going to be people who run faster, jump higher, dive deeper and come up drier."

Poet and songwriter Red Stegall says Royal should try his hand at another trade.

"Darrell really admires creative people; he admires the art form," Stegall said. "I think there is one thing he would

Royal and country-western singer Roy Clark.

118

Royal's home is often a site for country-western singers to perform: (left to right) Mickey Newburg, Larry Gatlin, Willie Nelson and Steve Gatlin.

love to do and has never done and that's write songs.

"He is not a country music fan; he is a country music fanatic. He grew up in rural Oklahoma and he relates to the lyrics of country music. He identifies with all those people we write about. They have been a part of his world at some time in his life."

The walls of the Royals' home are adorned with pictures of family and friends, famous or not. But there are no pictures of Royal in coaching garb. Perhaps the only object that relates to his past sits on the coffee table in the den — a wheel hub off an old Whippet automobile found some years ago by Edith on one of her antique shop forages. There is no trophy room in the Royal house.

To illustrate why, Royal tells the story of a trip he made to a one-night performance once with Willie Nelson. The mayor of the city had presented Nelson with a commemorative plaque, and as he and Willie walked from the small airport to board a chartered Lear jet, Darrell mentioned to Willie that he'd left the plaque on a table in the private waiting area. Nelson kept on walking.

"I said, 'Willie, how can you leave that plaque?' He said, 'You know, they enjoyed giving me that plaque and I appreciated it and really enjoyed getting it. But I'm not obligated to tote that son of a bitch around the rest of my life. I am not a slave to my possessions.'

"I feel pretty much the same way," Royal said. "So you don't see any trophies around here. I've moved them to other places."

In his 70's, Royal finds life easy to come to.

"I find that I have more emotions about situations than I used to," he said. "Like when they told me about the stadium being named for me. The older I get, the more I appreciate a compliment.

"When I was working and an honor or recognition

Royal was inducted into the College Football Hall of Fame in 1983.

A favorite of Royal's is Earnest Tubbs (right).

came my way, I didn't really believe it and I didn't really enjoy it because I knew I had to maintain — to go out and prove again that I deserved it. Now, I get a compliment and I appreciate it. I don't feel like I have to do anything to earn it again.

"The years fly faster. I don't feel my age — though I can tell the ball doesn't fly as far — and I think I compare favorably with people my age. I think I get around better than the average guy because I play golf all the time. I do a lot of brisk walking and I go to the spa where I work out and do a little light weightlifting. I feel good."

As Edith said, Royal appears at peace.

"I think Willie said it perfectly in one of his songs," Darrell said, " 'Yesterday's dead and tomorrow's blind. I live one day at a time.'

"And really, I think I've lived one period at a time. One day at a time now. The past is history. Sometimes, it's almost like I didn't coach. As involved and as intense as I was — and I was intense about it — after two or three years I unwound. And unwound, I'm pretty good at being lazy. I could give lessons in it.

"I tell people that I hope when they retire, they can enjoy it as much as I have."

Darrell Royal
Ten
to Remember

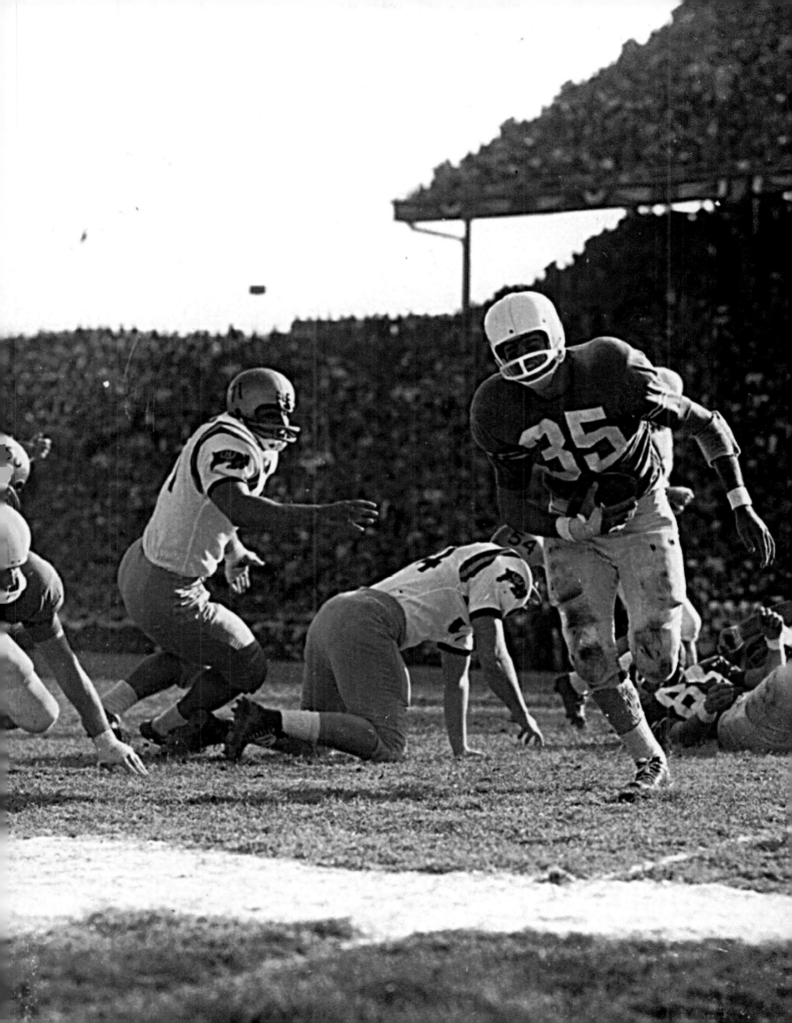

Spirited Longhorns Shade Sooners in Thriller

By Flem R. Hall
Fort Worth Star-Telegram

DALLAS, October 11, 1958

On the wings of spectacularly successful passing and that imponderable of football spirit, the University of Texas Longhorns soared to a 15-14 victory over the University of Oklahoma Sooners here this gray, cool Saturday afternoon to shatter a winning string that stretched through six of their annual games in the Cotton Bowl.

The Longhorns just wouldn't accept defeat.

With less than seven minutes left to play they found themselves the victims of a cruel turn of fumble-fate and trailing by six points, but instead of folding up, the Steers fought off the Big Red and countered with an attack that swirled 75 yards on 13 plays to mark the touchdown that tied the score at 14-14.

There was 3:10 to play when, with George Blanch holding, Bobby Lackey place-kicked the conversion point that won the game.

It was the brilliant passing of Vince Matthews, the No. 2 quarterback, that swept the Sooners to the brink of defeat, but it was Lackey who tossed the seven-yard jump pass that Bob Bryant caught in the end zone to tie the score.

Matthews completed six of eight passes for all the

Royal is carried off the field triumphantly by Longhorn linemen Harry Anderson (68) and Dan Petty (62).

yards except that last seven, on the decisive move.

Earlier in the game he hit 2-for-2 to bring his full game record to 8-of-10 for 126 yards.

It was against a panorama of a solid-packed, color-splashed crowd of 75,504 that the two rivals played as exciting a contest as any of the previous 52 games played since 1900.

Texas took the lead, 8-0, in the second quarter. Oklahoma scored in the third quarter, but missed a bid for two extra points and trailed 8-6 going into the fourth period.

Fighting with all the fury and cunning they could muster, the Longhorns stopped an Oklahoma drive and took the ball on downs in the third minute of the fourth quarter on the Texas 24.

Then came the day's strangest play.

On the first down, fullback Mike Dowdle fumbled when hit hard at the line of scrimmage by Jerry Thompson, the Oklahoma guard.

Jim Davis, the other Oklahoma guard, found the ball hanging like a ripe grape, plucked it out of the air as he rushed forward, burst into the open and lumbered untouched 24 yards for the quick touchdown that left Texas behind, 12-8.

It was enough to break the heart and resistance of a lesser team when, on top of that, Oklahoma added two points on a pass play that appeared dead before the ball was ever thrown, but Texas wasn't through, although trailing, 14-8.

George Blanch (41) and Bob Bryant (85) both caught key passes in one of the Longhorns' scoring drives.

The Longhorns rallied first to keep the fired-up Sooners from rushing across a clinching touchdown. Then Texas stuck back with as pretty a passing display as you will ever see.

Lackey was taken out of the game after he received an Oklahoma punt and returned six yards to the Texas 25.

Matthews was fresh and armed to strike at the Sooners' vulnerable secondary where only Jake Sandefer had been consistently effective against passes.

On first down Matthews passed to Bryant for five yards. Then a running play with Bobby Matocha carrying made six. Matthews hit Rene Ramirez deep over the middle for 12 yards. Then he switched to Bryant, who was on his knees when he scooped the pass into his arms just before it hit the ground.

That made it first down on the OU 41.

For variety, Matthews called a halfback pass, but the would-be passer, Blanch, was tackled for an eight-yard loss without getting rid of the ball.

Matthews then missed on a shot, too high for Maurice Doke.

With third and 18 yards needed, Matthews first hit Blanch for 11 yards and then Bryant for seven and the first down, by inches on the 30.

Still hot and accurate, the tall junior quarterback from Houston passed to Ramirez, who appeared gone for a touchdown until Sandefer downed him on the 19 with a leaping tackle.

The Sooners loosened their defense and when they did Matthews sent Dowdle blasting through the middle for 14 yards.

1958 University of Texas Longhorns.

When a fumble lost two yards and a pass went incomplete, Longhorns coach Darrell Royal replaced Matthews with Lackey.

He came in with the right play — a quick pass over the center of the line to Bryant, who was open as a butcher knife, and across the line for the six points that tied the score at 14.

The winning point was quick, slick and perfect, with Capt. Arlis Parkhurst centering the ball; Blanch holding and Lackey kicking.

Actually it was the failure to convert after their first touchdown that ultimately defeated the Sooners. Trying for an 8-8 tie they went for two points by passing, but Bobby Boyd's pass to Jerry Tillery bit into the grass before it reached either the receiver or the goal line.

In addition to the time they scored, each team made only one serious scoring threat. Texas thrust 57 yards to the OU 4 in the last minute of the first quarter and was still there when a fourth-down incomplete pass killed the move on the first play of the second quarter.

Oklahoma rushed 50 yards to the Texas 5 in the third quarter when Matocha broke.

Texas was trying to get out of that corner when a short punt gave the Sooners another shot from the 38. That time they made it. Jimmy and Dick Carpenter (both from West Texas but unrelated), Boyd and David Rolle, all the reserves, carried the drive. It was Dick Carpenter who fled around right end for the last five yards and the touchdown.

The Sooners mustered a mild threat in the second quarter, after Texas scored, by moving 61 yards to the 12, but it was fourth and seven when Ronnie Hartline tried a field goal from the 20 at a slight angle. The kick was long and high enough but a bit wide to the left.

So altogether OU was on the Texas 12, 23, 5 and 24 without scoring.

Even after Texas had scored the winning point, Oklahoma took the kickoff and with wild and desperate plays got to the Texas 44, before Lackey broke the threat with a pass interception on the side line at the Texas 28. From there, with a minute left, the Longhorns ran out the clock while losing ground with delaying plays.

The last big thrill of the game came during that final Oklahoma bid when Boyd, trying to pass, ran back and forth across the field away from rushers until he found running room and blockers. Then he zigzagged 26 yards before being pulled down by Larry Stephens when it looked as if Boyd might go all the way.

SCORE BY QUARTERS

Texas	0	8	0	7	—	15
Oklahoma	0	0	6	8	—	14

Jerry Cook (38) intercepts Ole Miss quarterback Doug Elmore's (15) pass near the goal line. Cook would finish the afternoon with a Cotton Bowl-record three interceptions.

Texas Interceptions Jar Ole Miss Attack

By Bill Van Fleet
Fort Worth Star-Telegram

DALLAS, January 1, 1962

The Texas Longhorns built a 12-0 halftime lead off Mississippi's boomeranging pass attack, then fought off the Rebels through the final two periods to win the Cotton Bowl game Monday, 12-7.

It was a spectacular performance by the underdog Longhorns, who were scrapping against an equally spectacular Mississippi team.

The Longhorns, who entered this game with great respect for the fearsome Rebel passing attack, grabbed four interceptions in the first half and one of them led directly to the game's first touchdown.

Another interception quenched a Mississippi threat at the Texas seven just before the halftime gun.

It was the Rebels' turn to do the intercepting in the second half, and they grabbed three of Mike Cotten's aerials while completing enough of their own to keep the pressure on the Longhorns.

They scored one touchdown on a 20-yard pass, and reached deep Texas territory one other time.

The raging contest lived up to its advance billing as the most interesting bowl game of the year, and the Cotton Bowl throng of nearly 80,000 was kept in an uproar.

The official, paid attendance was 75,504, capacity of the big bowl, but Howard Grubbs, the executive secretary of the Southwest Conference, said band members,

ushers and workers added about 5,000 to that total.

The Longhorn secondary came in for a shower of praise for the alertness of the pass defense, but actually it was an outweighed Texas line which forced Mississippi to turn almost exclusively to the air after the first few moments. Ole Miss never was able to mount a sustained land drive.

The Rebels threw 37 times and completed only 15, while having five passes intercepted.

Big Jerry Cook, the junior tailback, grabbed three of the Rebel passes and Pat Culpepper and Tommy Ford intercepted one each.

Texas had its defensive halfbacks spread a little wide most of the day, as precaution against "sprint out" passes, and at times the Longhorns abandoned their normal wide tackle six defense to go into a four-four.

The tactics were successful.

Ole Miss was held to 127 yards on the ground and gained 192 more in the air for a total offense of 319 yards, well below the team's season norm.

The Rebels were just as tough as the Longhorns on defense most of the day, but they were cracked on a 34-yard ground surge for the first touchdown in the opening period and in the second. Quarterback Cotten and wingback Jack Collins worked a beautiful pass-run play for 24 yards and the other Texas touchdown.

For his great first-half performance, Cotten was voted the game's outstanding back.

Teammate Bob Moses drew the outstanding lineman award. His hard tackle on Glynn Griffing on a crucial fourth-down play at the Texas 23 late in the game no doubt was the big vote-getter.

The tackle threw Griffing for a one-yard loss, and left Moses so stunned he had to leave the game.

Texas came up with some surprises on offense, too. Collins, the wingback, was flanked wide to one side or another, and several times tailback James Saxton went sprinting out in his direction to take a long flat throw from Cotten.

The play worked well, and helped scatter the Rebel defense. Fullback Ray Poage, returning to the Texas lineup as a full-time offensive performer for the first time since October, was the game's leading rusher with 54 yards.

The Rebels, who already had lost their starting fullback when Billy Ray Adams was injured in an early December car wreck, saw the No. 1 substitute, Buck Randall, go out with a knee injury in the second period. The third stringer, Fred Roberts, played the second half.

Alan Baum turns the corner on the Ole Miss defense.

The Longhorns had their share of good luck through the day, but their first big break did not pay off. In fact, Ole Miss looked like a winner on that exchange.

It happened on the second play of the game. Doug Elmore, the senior Rebel quarterback fumbled, and Eddie Padgett recovered for the Longhorns at the Mississippi 26.

But a furious defense stopped Texas on three plays and when a field-goal try by Eldon Moritz was short, there must have been a wave of doubt sweeping over the many Texas supporters.

The Rebels took over at their 10, where the field-goal try expired, and overcame two five-yard penalties in moving out of the Texas 44.

Cook started his intercepting then, grabbing an Elmore pass at the 25 and running it back to the Texas 33.

The Longhorns couldn't move and punted over the goal, but Ford made his interception at the Rebel 34, shortly thereafter, and the Longhorns quickly moved into touchdown land.

Culpepper, almost exclusively a defensive hand, rambled for 12 yards to the 22 on a pitchout to start the drive.

Saxton got two yards, and Poage skipped to the left on a pitchout for nine more to set up first down at the 11.

With Saxton lending a good block, Poage picked up five of the six yards. David Russell went flying to the left on a reverse, but was bumped out on the one-foot line, where it was first down.

Cotten got a couple of inches, then Saxton rammed his head over right tackle for enough for the touchdown.

Big Jim Dunaway blocked the point try by Moritz.

The second Texas touchdown was more spectacular, and the 72-yard drive had people wondering if the Longhorns were going to make a runaway of the contest. It came 10 minutes deep into the second period.

Duke Carlisle, an alert and aggressive defender all afternoon made a fair catch at the Texas 28 to start things.

Poage ran for four yards and Cotten hit Saxton with two straight passes to set up a first down at the 39. Cotten fell victim to a Rebel rush and lost three, but on the next play he fooled the rushers by keeping and darting into the clear. He kept going for 27 yards and a first down at the Mississippi 37.

Saxton got two yards, then gave way to Ford, who caught a swing pass for a 12-yard gain. Poage lost a yard back to the 24, but on second down Cotten passed to Collins at about the 16.

The senior wingback did a beautiful job of running and finally out-raced Rebel defenders down the sideline for the touchdown. Collins tried to run for two points, but was stopped a yard short.

The Rebels came charging back and moved from their own 23 to a first down at the Texas 7 just before the half ended.

Griffing tried a pass from there, and Johnny Treadwell upped it into the air. Cook ran under it, and the threat was over as Cotten ran out the remaining 55 seconds.

The Rebels made another big move at the start of the second half, but Cook again broke that one up with an interception.

The Rebels now turned to the interception game, and the ball was traded twice before a Mississippi punt died at the Texas 13.

The Longhorns took time out and when the referee signaled for play to start again, they rushed out of the huddle quickly, with Saxton in short punt formation. He kicked one that rolled all the way to the Ole Miss 14 before it died.

That great play, however, seemed to make the Rebs more determined and they went 36 yards for the score, in just eight plays.

Big plays were a keeper by Griffing, who darted 29 yards to the Texas 20, and the touchdown pass from Griffing to Reed Davis. David Russell had Davis covered, but he made a fine catch.

When Wes Sullivan kicked the extra point, there was 3:35 left in the third period.

The Longhorns put on one of their characteristic rallies on the next kickoff, surging all the way to the Mississippi 8, but a third pass was intercepted, and Texas was through threatening.

The Rebs had one big drive left, however. Starting from their own 46, they moved to a first down at the Texas 31. A pass gained to the 25, a run got two more yards. End Woody Dabbs had a pass within his clutch hands at the 11, but Carlisle smacked him in time and the ball rolled free.

On fourth down, Griffing started rolling out on the option, but Moses smacked him for a yard loss and the threat was over.

The game ended with the ball in midfield.

The victory was a sweet one for Darrell Royal, the young coach of the Longhorns. It was his first bowl victory since he has been at Texas, although his team played a 3-3 tie with Alabama in the Bluebonnet Bowl last year.

The victory wiped out memories of a 39-7 defeat Mississippi handed Royal's first Texas team after the 1957 season in the Sugar Bowl.

SCORE BY QUARTERS

Mississippi	0	0	7	0	—	7
Texas	6	6	0	0	—	12

Late Texas Thrust Spears Hogs

By Bill Van Fleet

Fort Worth Star-Telegram

AUSTIN, October 20, 1962

With just 36 seconds showing on the clock, tailback Tommy Ford shot through the left side of the stubbornly fighting Arkansas defense for three yards and a touchdown that gave Texas a 7-3 victory in one of the all-time great Southwest Conference games Saturday night.

The Memorial Stadium crowd of 64,530 had been steadily approaching insanity as a drive that had been launched from the Texas 15 moved laboriously toward the Arkansas goal.

With first Duke Carlisle and then John Genung directing, the move crossed midfield and then the Longhorns began a series of cliff-hangers.

Twice they needed a fourth down to set up a new series, and once Jerry Cook got the yardage and the other time Genung passed to Ford to reach the 14.

Three plays set up another first down at the four, and now there was 1:27 on the clock.

Ford got a yard, but sophomore Stan Sparks slapped away Genung's pass on the next play and the excitement was almost unbearable.

Ford, a determined runner all night, got the call on a power sweep and he went barreling in with room to spare.

There was time left for the kickoff, which Tony Crosby sent out of the end zone, and one Arkansas play. That was a long pass by sophomore Billy Gray, and Longhorns Carlisle and Joe Dixon came down with it in joint grasp at the Texas 44.

The victorious players just stood and waited as the clock ran out the final few seconds.

The pressure of the finish was too much for one spectator, who dashed out on the field and connected with a good punch to the head of referee Curly Hays before Don Jester, a former Austin Golden Gloves champion, separated the pair.

It was the kind of ball game that neither team should have lost. The Razorbacks, fighting with every ounce of their energy, had established 3-0 lead in the second period on sophomore

Tom McKnelly's 41-yard field goal, and they had narrowly missed scoring again when fullback Danny Brabham fumbled into the end zone as he tried to drive across from the three.

Dixon scooped the ball to his bosom there, and Texas escaped that threat, only to give the Razorbacks one more chance with a fumble at the Longhorn 21 three plays later.

That move was smothered on fourth down at the 12 by the raging Johnny Treadwell, a great guard for Texas on this night, and the rest of the game belonged to Texas.

The Longhorns, too, had their first-half chances, but

Duke Carlisle (11) sweeps wide on an option play against the Arkansas defense.

one move died at the seven when Carlisle was caught for no gain on a rollout, and a Texas field goal missed from the 31 as time ran out at intermission.

The statistics reveal just how close the game was. Texas made 13 first downs against 12, but the Razorbacks held a slight total yardage edge, 215 to 204. Curiously, both teams launched the same number of plays (64).

One big factor was penalties. The Longhorns managed to play the 60 minutes without drawing even a five-yard fine, while the Razorbacks were assessed four 15-yarders.

The kicking Ernie Koy, a Texas sophomore, again was long and accurate, and he wound up the night with an average of 43.8 on six punts.

It was a kick by Tommy Moore, the Razorback punting specialist, which seemed likely to be the decisive play until the Texas comeback in the fourth.

Moore lifted a high one that rolled and bounded and finally died on the Texas two early in the second.

Texas couldn't move it and Koy kicked high to the Texas 49. From there, the Razorbacks posted two first downs to reach the 24 before the furiously fighting Longhorns stopped them.

Two plays by swift Jesse Branch got three yards to the 22, and sophomore end Knox Nunnally drove quarterback Billy Moore back to the 24 on the third down.

McKnelly came in, and with the ball spotted on the 31, drove it 41 yards straight and high through the goal markers.

Texas, with Koy making two big runs, provided all the threats in the rest of the first half, but as related, all failed.

The Texas supporters in the big crowd had never given up, nor ceased their uproar, but when the Longhorns gained possession on their own 15 after a fair catch by Carlisle, midway in the fourth it represented the final chance for a comeback.

The clock showed 7:55 left, and the Razorback goal was 85 rugged yards away.

Carlisle, who had started the game, was thrown for a five-yard loss back to the 10 on the first play.

The junior quarterback, who also is a defensive specialist, then hit Tommy Lucas for 12 yards. He needed three big yards on fourth down, and he passed to end Sandy Sands for 11 and a first down at the 33.

The Texan cannon, usually reserved for touchdowns, boomed out the first shot of what was to become a veritable cannonade as the Longhorns kept on making the big play.

Carlisle came right back with another pass to Sands for 14 yards and a first down at the 47, and the cannon boomed again.

Carlisle, with his receivers covered, tried two keepers and got a total of five yards — and there it was again, third down with sizable yardage needed. He called on the burly Cook, who fought and twisted to near the first-down spot.

When the officials brought out the chain, it was short by a foot.

Genung came in then, and the rest of the drive belonged to him. He sent Cook driving and churning into the Arkansas right side, and he got two yards to set up a first down at the 42. The cannon blasted again.

Cook was hot, and he got the call again, picking up five yards.

Then came the game's biggest break. Genung rolled out to his right and threw a flat pass.

Sparks intercepted it, but one foot was out of bounds by inches and Texas kept possession. That interpretation by the referee brought another shot from the delirious cannoneers.

Genung tried to run to the left, but he was caught after a yard gain, and it was third and four.

The quarterback sent end Charley Talbert racing across the middle and hit him for a 10-yard pass that set up first down and brought another shot.

By now everybody was standing and yelling defiance or encouragement, and only 3:02 showed on the clock.

Fullback Ray Poage blasted for four yards, and Ford got three more to the 19.

Genung now sent Ford down the left side, and hit the stubby, hard-nosed, little runner with another completion just before he was swarmed under by raging Arkansas defenders.

The cannon almost blew itself apart.

With 2:12 still showing, Genung passed to Talbert for eight more yards to the 6. Texas took time to stop the clock, and then Poage rooted for two yards to set a measured first down. The cannon cut loose.

Genung called on Ford who could get but one yard, and the alert Sparks batted away a pass to Talbert, as the cannon mechanics held their fire.

The next play was to be the last chance for victory, for undoubtedly the Longhorns would have gone for a field goal and a tie if it had failed.

Ford came blasting through on the power sweep as if he himself had been charged with the cannon's black powder, and the referee's hands went up.

Crosby's extra point was only a bit of gloss on a great victory.

The Texas triumph left the Longhorns as the favorite to win, or at lest share, a second consecutive league title — although they still have five SWC games to play.

SCORE BY QUARTERS

Arkansas	0	3	0	0	—	3
Texas	0	0	0	7	—	7

Longhorns Shock Oklahoma

By Jim Trinkle

Fort Worth Star-Telegram

DALLAS, October 12, 1963

Never did a team travel so far and gain so little ground as did Texas on Saturday with a 28-7 victory over Oklahoma that rearranged the national football rankings.

The Longhorns, No. 2 in the country when the 75,504 Cotton Bowl spectators took their seats, uncoiled a savage ground attack that accounted for 239 yards and three touchdowns.

Yet, when it was all over, when chaos had become mere bedlam among hysterical patrons of the Orange, Texas had, by any measurement, advanced only one peg.

But what a leap the one rung on the gridiron ladder represented.

The chant rose and swelled and boomed — "We're No. 1" — even before the Longhorns had added an aerial coup de grace to the demise of the Sooners, who had enjoyed the No. 1 ranking for two weeks.

The Longhorns left their feet only three times, and it was

the third one from reserve quarterback Marvin Kristynik to end George Sauer Jr. that drove the last nail in OU's coffin.

For the most part it was Texas' angry infantry, stung by its underdog role against a club it had beaten five previous years, that left the Big Red defense in ribbons.

Other Longhorn touchdowns were made by quarterback Duke Carlisle, tailback Tommy Ford and wingback Phil Harris as the Texas assault produced results in every period. Tony Crosby performed faultlessly as the extra-point hireling.

Oklahoma got its only touchdown in the third period when quarterback John Hammond ran three yards. Ralph Jarman kicked the extra point.

Texas went in front in the seventh minute of the first period — driving 68 yards against the team that two Saturdays ago had replaced Southern California as the boss of

college football — and was never headed.

At intermission, the Sooners could show only three first downs and a 77-yard overall production against the Longhorns' 11 first downs and 144 yards, all rushing.

The Texas line, stimulated by the tremendous effort of tackle Scott Appleton, repeatedly threw back the Oklahoma racehorses — Joe Don Looney, Jim Grisham and Lance Rentzel.

Grisham performed creditably with 74 yards on nine carries — second only to Ford's 77 in 21 attempts — but behind the Sooner fullback, the ground gains fell away to Rentzel's 18 yards.

Behind Ford for the Orange footmen came Carlisle, playing 34 minutes of the game with 62 yards.

It was the swift Texas quarterback, who reached his peak when nothing less would win, who ground out most of the yardage in the Longhorns' opening drive. Of the 13 plays in the 68-yard sortie, he called his own number on six of them and pricked the OU defense for 37 yards.

On the second play of the game, the little senior blared to his left then swerved into the Sooner midsection for 14 yards before Midland's Carl Schreiner could spill him. If this was to be the pattern of the day, Texas' backs traced it beautifully.

Ford got his licks in for 19 yards in the big move, but it was Carlisle on three consecutive stabs who got the final seven yards.

Oklahoma got in only six offensive plays in the first period, and one of them was a pass by quarterback Bob Page that fell into defender Pete Lammons' grasp.

Texas took this ownership and nearly squeezed six points from it. John Porterfield crashed in on fourth down to turn back Carlisle when Duke needed only two yards for a touchdown.

An 18-yard punt return by Tony King and a personal-foul penalty against the Sooners prodded Texas into

motion the next time the ball changed hands. The Longhorns only had to move 22 yards, and in three plays Ford and Carlisle had them.

Ford, running with his nose close to the ground, swirled through his left tackle and nobody could stop him. Jackey Cowan tried on the goal line and got his britches dusted for his trouble.

Oklahoma made its first venture across midfield — its previous time in Texas territory came on a short Longhorn punt — just before the half, but the clock caught the Sooners on the UT 45.

The Big Red's finest moments came in the third quarter, but not until Carlisle and Harris had collaborated on a three-yard touchdown in the first five minutes.

It appeared to be a flair pass as Duke swung out of his blocks and whipped the ball overhand to Harris, who fled to the corner for the touchdown. Texas statisticians insisted, however, the flip was a lateral. Whatever it was, it carried a six-point label.

Then it was Oklahoma's part. The Sooners crashed 62 yards —their longest exploration of the day — with Hammond passing twice to Allen Bumgardner and Rick McCurdy for first downs. The one to Bumgardner covered 17 yards, and 11 to McCurdy. Grisham pounded through the middle for 14 yards, but Hammond kept for the last stride.

Nobody had held the Big Eight champions to a single touchdown since Texas won the 1952 game here, 9-6. And it appeared the Sooners might get another one until Grisham, who had just run 31 yards to Texas' 43, fumbled four plays later.

Oklahoma didn't know it, but it wasn't to get the ball for but two more plays. They were after Longhorns coach Darrell Royal had inserted a new team directed by Kristynik into the game.

The Baytown sophomore took them 63 yards in 11 calls, whipping a 14-yard pass to Sauer for the last touchdown.

Charley Talbert (89) attempts to tackle Oklahoma's Rick McCurdy (80).

SCORE BY QUARTERS

Oklahoma	0	0	7	0	—	7
Texas	7	7	7	7	—	28

No. 1 Longhorns Sink No. 2 Navy

By Bill Van Fleet

Fort Worth Star-Telegram

DALLAS, January 1, 1964

All hail the mighty Texas Longhorns! They proved with a deadly finality that they are champions of all college football, in all sections of the country and even in television land, by smashing Navy, 28-6, in the 1964 Cotton Bowl game Wednesday afternoon.

The Longhorns have been rated No. 1 since they beat Oklahoma by a similar score (28-7) in mid-October, but there were doubters until this spectacular game.

There can be none now. The Texans whipped the No. 2 Middies thoroughly, running up a 21-0 advantage at halftime, boosting it to 28-0 in the third. They gave up a score only after a mixture of second- and third-stringers took the field.

The final gun caught Texas on the Navy one-foot line, vainly striving for a fifth touchdown.

The method of the victory was almost as startling as the margin, for Texas came out throwing and kept it up until the game was safely tucked away.

The hero was not Roger Staubach, the Navy's all-America quarterback and passing star.

That honor went to Duke Carlisle, the slender Texas quarterback who had been regarded as only a so-so passer all season. Carlisle threw two tremendous touchdown passes to the swift gaited Phil Harris, a sophomore wingback, to build up a 14-0 margin in the first 20 minutes then ran nine yards for the third touchdown seven minutes later.

Harold Philipp found a big hole at the left side and ran two yards for the final touchdown, with 12 minutes gone in the third.

Navy got its score three minutes deep in the fourth when Staubach merely strolled around his right end for two yards after faking a pass.

Carlisle's two touchdown passes covered 58 and 63 yards, respectively, with Harris out-fighting Navy's Pat Donnelly for the ball both times, then doing some fancy running to go the rest of the way.

The game was played in a splendid setting, with a bright sun lighting the field and the temperature 45 degrees at kickoff. The Cotton Bowl was jammed with perhaps 78,000 people. All the 75,504 seats were sold, and workers and bandsmen added to the throng.

While Carlisle led the offense, the giant Scott Appleton captained an almost flawless performance by the Texas defense.

When the game was over, the Middies had minus-14 yards rushing, and while Staubach set a new Cotton Bowl passing record by completing 21 of 31 for 223 yards, he could never connect on a scoring heave.

The Texas linemen were quick as cats as they poured after Staubach. They also protected the middle fiercely and stopped the traps and draw plays that Navy had used with success through the regular season. Navy never made a first down rushing. The Middies made 14 by passing and two on Texas penalties for a total of 16. Texas had 18, getting nine rushing and eight passing.

GAME 5 Texas vs. Navy, 1964 Cotton Bowl

Duke Carlisle (11) set a Cotton Bowl record with 213 yards passing for two TD's and 54 yards rushing.

Carlisle, the man they said could not pass, picked the Navy defense expertly.

At the start of the game, he found the eager Middies stacking the Texas inside game but on third down he loped to his left, faked a pass, and ran 19 yards for a first down.

After that, a running play failed and he overshot Harris on his first pass try. On the next try, he took a step to left, caught the Navy defenders moving with what they thought was the flow of the play, stopped and quickly passed across field to Harris. The sophomore beat Donnelly on the catch, kept his footing and at the 16-yard line faked defender Robert Sutton into a futile dive. He flashed on across.

Texas, for the eighth time this season, had scored on its first possession. Furthermore, Carlisle had found the key to the Navy defense.

The rest of the afternoon he kept starting plays by taking a step in one direction to draw the Navy defense, then either passing or handing back to a teammate going into the other side of the line.

When the senior from Athens finally left the game for good in the third period, he was given a tumultuous ovation.

While he was in there, Carlisle completed seven of 19 passes for 213 yards and ran for a net of 54 — giving him a new total offense record of 267 yards for the Cotton Bowl. There's no estimating what his total would have been had he played the final 23 minutes against the tiring Navy team.

When Duke left the game he also owned a new record for passing yardage, his 213 surpassing the 174 Chuck Curtis of TCU gained against Syracuse in 1957.

Staubach erased that mark, however, for he kept

139

chucking and wound up with 228 yards.

The relentless Texas defenders rushed Staubach with such ferocity that he wound up losing 47 yards on the ground.

Carlisle was voted the game's outstanding back, receiving 95 of 100 votes cast. Harris got four, and there was one lone holdout for Staubach.

Appleton led the vote for outstanding lineman with Tommy Nobis, George Brucks and Charles Talbert, all of Texas, finishing in that order. Navy's Charles Durepo and Dave Sjuggerud each got one vote from the press box, which was filled with writers from all over the country.

The Longhorns used their ends to put outside pressure on Staubach and contain him.

Frequently, Staubach resorted to safety valve or swing passes, but each time the receiver found a Longhorn nearby and the gains were negligible. Often the receivers were hit by crackling tackles.

After the Longhorns marched 78 yards to their first touchdown, they were halted on their next three possessions. Five minutes deep in the second, Joe Ince kicked the ball dead to the Texas 37.

On the first play, Carlisle started to his right, whirled and passed to Harris at the Navy 38. Donnelly tipped the ball, and seemed about to intercept it when Harris stole it. The sophomore came down, kept his feet and with Charley Talbert screening off the last defender, fled down the sidelines and across the goal.

A Navy fumble at its 34 set up the third Texas drive. Staubach was hit by Clayton Lacy as he tried to run wide and Bobby Gamblin fell on the ball.

A five-yard penalty set Texas back to the 39, but seven plays later Carlisle, following sophomore guard Frank Bedrick, went twisting on a nine-yard run to touchdown. Tony Crosby kicked the third of his four points and it was 21-0.

The final touchdown drive covered 53 yards. Tommy Wade came in to relieve the tiring Carlisle when the ball was on the 26, and straight-a-way he threw a 21-yard pass to sophomore George Sauer.

Tommy Ford got three yards and then Philipp found enough running room for a whole squad to pour through as he got the touchdown.

Navy put on its only successful drive after that, moving 75 yards after the kickoff. Two five-yard penalties near the goal helped the Middies.

In addition to their four touchdowns, the Longhorns fouled up a fake field goal in the first period and Crosby missed a 22-yard field goal try in the third.

A Texas football team was never sharper than the one which won Wednesday. The players seemed to do everything right.

Typical was Kim Gaynor, the slight sophomore who was pressed in as a punter after Ernie Koy was hurt early in the season. The Castleberry High graduate averaged 32.6 yards through the regular season, but on his three kicks against Navy he averaged 43.3. One of them was a booming 48-yarder into the slight wind.

Records fell all around. As mentioned before, Carlisle's 267 yards total offense is a new one, wiping out the 265 yards Dicky Moegle of Rice made rushing against Alabama in 1954. First Carlisle, then Staubach went past Curtis' record of 174 yards passing.

Skip Orr, who caught nine, removed the old mark of eight catches by Hub Bechtol of Texas against Missouri in 1946 and Tee Moorman of Duke against Arkansas in 1961.

When Harris caught the two touchdown passes, he tied with L.D. Meyer of TCU (1937), Joe Bill Baumgardner of Texas (1946) and Emery Clark of Kentucky (1952).

Staubach's 21 completions wiped out the old mark of 13 held jointly by Frank Ryan of Rice and Tom Forrestal of Navy.

On the debit side, Navy's minus-14 yards rushing tied the record held by Tennessee since 1953. Texas also furnished the defense that time.

Navy's 22 completions (Donnelly threw one to Staubach) erased the old mark of 15 set by Mississippi in the 1962 game with Texas.

SCORE BY QUARTERS

Navy	0	0	0	6	—	6
Texas	7	14	7	0	—	28

Texas Stuns No. 1 Alabama With Long Bombs

By Jim Trinkle
Fort Worth Star-Telegram

MIAMI, Fla., January 1, 1965

With the new year still in the maternity ward and Alabama reeling from a 21-17 defeat, Texas became king for a day before 72,647 Orange Bowl spectators Friday night.

It doesn't count, really, not the claim to royalty. But the four-point victory over the 1964 national champions does, erected in one of the genuine scoring thrillers of all 31 of these Jan. 1 classics.

Texas led all the way. The Longhorns, ranked fifth and a three-point underdog to the Crimson Tide, got a two-touchdown swirl from tailback Ernie Koy — one of a record-setting journey — and slammed the door on Alabama's furious finish just inches from the Texas goal.

At the game's end on the rain-slickened Orange Bowl turf, the Longhorns owned the ball near mid-field. They weren't about to give it up.

Joe Namath, Alabama's lamelegged quarterback, played a mag-

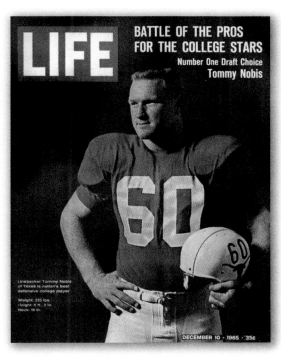

nificent game on a leg that allegedly was no stronger than one of Grandma Clampitt's. He was voted the most valuable player award for passing for both of Alabama's touchdowns.

He completed 18 passes — a new record — out of 37 tries for 255 yards.

Koy also shattered a long-standing mark with a 79-yard run that sent Texas winging to its victory. The old record had lasted since Ned Peters of Mississippi dashed 67 yards against Catholic University in 1936.

He later rumbled over from a yard out and Jim Hudson, on his first play in the game, threw a 69-yard pass to end George Sauer for the other Texas touchdown. David Conway kicked all three extra points.

Namath and Steve Sloan, who started as the Tide's offensive marshal, flung the ball around like a hot potato. They accounted for 298 yards and their 44 aerials was another new entry in the Orange Bowl ledger.

The touchdown tosses covered seven yards to Wayne Trimble and 20 yards to end Ray Perkins, who was a particular

pain to Texas defenders in the first major bowl game ever played under lights. David Ray added a 26-yard field goal and two points-after-touchdown.

The Longhorns' turbulent defense, led by linebacker Tommy Nobis and assisted by Frank Bedrick, Olen Underwood, Clayton Lacy, Diron Talbert and Knox Nunnally, surrendered only 49 yards rushing to the Alabama travelers.

Texas got 212 yards, but it was the ring-a-ding dash by Koy that made all the others pale by comparison.

Alabama made the first offensive threat but Ray's 45-yard field-goal attempt fell short, giving Texas possession on the 20. Fullback Harold Philipp could budge Alabama's thorny line for only a yard on quarterback Marvin Kristynik's call. Then Koy, who now can wring a handsome dowry from his courtiers in New York and Houston, thrashed around the right side of Texas line, broke free on the 40 and fled into the Alabama end zone.

Alabama coach Bear Bryant, recounting Koy's run and the long strike from Hudson to Sauer, said, "I don't ever remember any team scoring two long touchdowns against us like Texas did."

And Darrell Royal, the Texas coach, may not remember a more fierce defense by a Longhorn team than the one that hurled Alabama back in the last period.

A mental lapse by Kristynik on an attempted pass very nearly put Texas' early heroics into discard. About to be swarmed under, he flipped the ball free, where it was batted into Jim Fuller's hands on the Longhorn 34.

Almost 10 minutes remained in the game and Texas owned the same margin it finished with. Namath passed 16 yards to Ray Ogden and 13 to fullback Steve Bowman. Then he started dispatching Bowman into the Texas belly.

On three straight thrusts starting at the 6-yard line he got four, none and one yards. Then it was fourth and one and Namath, tired of this foolishness, flung himself into the tiger's mouth.

Nobis spit him back out, and when the officials ruled he had not crossed over, the Alabama quarterback raved and ranted like a man gone mad. Matter of fact, he had,

without actually frothing.

Koy kicked the Steers out of peril, then Pete Lammons intercepted a pass to quash another attack, and finally Namath just couldn't find the receivers he had waiting on him most of the night.

It seemed as if each time Ray, Alabama's placement ace and the NCAA record-holder as a kicker, missed a boot, Texas scored.

He even missed from the 14, which would have been a 24-yarder if it hadn't veered off to the right. The ball was replaced on the 20 — and Texas went 80 yards. Eleven of these steps were under Kristynik's guidance.

Off the bench stepped Hudson, injured most of the year but an acknowledged passer of repute. He threw, and as the ball soared nearly 40 yards through Miami's moist atmosphere, Sauer ran his heart out. He and the ball arrived at the Alabama 23 at the same time. It settled in over Mickey Andrews' anxious mitts, and Sauer won the race to the goal.

Alabama came right back with an 87-yard march. Namath passed Texas dizzy, throwing to Perkins for 25 and nine yards, popping one into Tommy Tolleson's hands for 15 and another to Wayne Cook for nine. Then he nailed Trimble in the end zone to make it 14-7.

The Longhorns wiped the sweat from their eyes — it was 70 degrees — and brought it right back. The march went 72 yards and Koy swept around right end for the last yard with only 27 seconds left at the half.

The Alabamians looked like national champions coming back from the half-time recess. They rammed 63 yards on their first ownership — only six of them on the ground — then Namath rolled out and passed to Perkins, who fell backward into the end zone.

Just before the third period ended Namath — who played in cleatless shoes to take pressure off his leg — drove the Tide 38 yards to Texas' 10 and told Ray to live up to his reputation. He did, and when his 26-yard field goal hit the ground, Texas' lead had dwindled to only four points. It held up even against Namath's spectacular passing, on that grinding defense Texas threw up at its goal.

Upon the Longhorns' arrival in Miami, Royal is greeted by Orange Bowl queen Linda Egland.

SCORE BY QUARTERS

Texas	7	14	0	0	—	21
Alabama	0	7	7	3	—	17

Longhorns Shoot Down Hogs

By Jim Trinkle
Fort Worth Star-Telegram

FAYETTEVILLE, Ark., December 6, 1969

And still college football's No. 1 team: The Texas Longhorns. Shaken from its doldrums with a 42-yard touchdown by James Street, Texas plunged past Arkansas in the last period Saturday to win the Southwest Conference championship.

In a typical chaotic fashion associated with this series, the Orange overcame the Razorbacks, 15-14, with a final surge witnessed by 50 million TV quarterbacks and President Nixon.

Even Billy Graham couldn't save Arkansas on Saturday. But for most of a long, leaden afternoon the Longhorns played as if the celebrated parson was calling their

Rooster Andrews and the Longhorns' sideline celebrates Jim Bertelsen's game-winning TD.

plays instead of sitting on the Razorback bench.

They fumbled on the second play of the game. Arkansas scored on the seventh.

So completely did Arkansas restrain the nation's No. 1 rushing team that Texas had gotten no closer than the Porker 31-yard line before Street's inspired dash on the first play of the fourth period.

Meanwhile, Bill Montgomery was frisking Texas' defense like a subway pickpocket. He did a marvelous job of third-down quarterbacking, sent Bill Burnett across from the one for Arkansas' first score, then passed to Chuck Dicus in the third quarter for what appeared an unassailable lead.

But Texas came back. As it had done through nine earlier games this year, it did what it had to do. Maybe there were a couple of miracles along the way — including a dazzling 44-yard reception by Randy Peschel — but when you're good, you make your miracles.

Street, unbeaten in his last 19 starts as Texas' quarterback, got the two-point conversion that gave the scoreboard the last unquenchable evidence of Texas' national rank.

He knifed in to shrink Arkansas' lead to 14-8. Then on a fourth-and-three emergency at his own 43, he collected Texas' gamble by nailing Peschel with the pass that stunned the Porkers. Two plays later Jim Bertelsen crunched across from two yards, and Happy Feller's place-kick wrote the final count.

It was a mournful ending to Arkansas' gallant stand. While Texas is playing Notre Dame in Dallas on Jan. 1, the Porkers will be salving their wounds in the Sugar Bowl against Mississippi. For 45 minutes, before a chilled gallery of 44,000, they deserved better.

Here were the Orange assassins, No. 2 in the nation in scoring with a 44-point average, and they couldn't make small change against Cliff Powell, Ricky Kersey, Lynn Garner and Arkansas' other defensive butchers.

The backfield that personally had outgained 85 major colleges was being held to a bunch of two-yard jabs.

And Montgomery was surrounded with a platoon of pass guardians who wouldn't let the Longhorns in. Well, the Razorbacks were No. 2 and like Texas as unblemished as the Astroturf.

They weren't expected to swoon, though bookmakers said they weren't within 11 points of Texas.

Arkansas kept Cotton Speyrer, Texas' explosive split end, pretty well harnessed. They didn't let Steve Worster of Bertelsen or Ted Koy get away on any fanciful voyages. But they couldn't pin Street's shoulders.

"He made the two big plays for them," Arkansas coach Frank Broyles said after the game. "He broke two tackles on his run, and he's quick."

"One of the great games of all time," President Nixon said in Texas' dressing room. Darrell Royal — who respects the Chief Executive's judgment — wasn't about to dispute him.

But when Texas faced second down eight yards shy of midfield, Royal was a lot closer to a holiday in New Orleans than in Dallas. His mood was one to match the dreary day.

But Street bounced off two tacklers, zigged as Terry Stewart zagged and outran the Arkansas defensive back

Mike Campbell, a longtime assistant to Royal, whose defense stopped the Razorbacks.

to the corner of the end zone. Thirteen seconds had passed in the last quarter.

"We stayed up till 1 o'clock talking about that two-point conversion," Royal said. Anyway, Street wheeled to his left and cut back in for the two-pointer.

If the touchdown raised Texas' spirits — and it did — Montgomery quickly turned to sinking them again. He kept tailback Burnett busy, and Burnett didn't score 19 touchdowns twiddling this thumbs.

And Dicus, the all-America end, was spearing passes from all angles. He caught three for 18, 20, and 21 but the first was canceled by a penalty. Then Montgomery had the Razorbacks only seven steps from Texas' goal and you could have bought Texas' national championship for a thin dime.

Maybe it was a bonehead play, since Montgomery had been fleecing Texas all afternoon with his keepers. But he passed. He passed to Dicus but Texas' Danny Lester never let it get to him. Dan roped it in the end zone and came out 20 yards.

Texas subsequently gave it back to 'em — just like Koy did on the game's second play when Arkansas scored — but the Porkers were never to get so close again.

Then it was Texas' game to win after taking Cary Stockdell's punt on its own 36. Koy could get only one yard and Worster was shut off with six in two calls.

Three yards were needed for a first down and the obvious play was a haymaker into the line or a razzoo at the flanks. The play came in from the bench.

"I called it," Royal said. "And I called it long." Long it was with Street heaving the ball almost 30 yards from the point of his retreat. Jerry Moore was hanging on Peschel like a Siamese twin. but the Longhorn end pulled down the ball with a falling catch on Arkansas' 13.

Koy got the first 11 and Bertelsen got the balance

over Bobby Mitchell's broad shoulder blades with only 3:58 left in the game. Feller did his job, and Frank Broyles' jaw sagged.

Still, there was time. As the parlor tacticians liberated a fresh six-pack at home, Montgomery brought Arkansas downfield again. The specter of Bill McClard kicking a long field goal must have chilled Royal. The Arkansas placement specialist has the range, and Montgomery was clicking.

It was race with time and Monty flicked his short ones to Burnett, who romanced the sidelines perfectly. They covered 11 and nine and seven yards, and Burnett flung himself across the Texas line on a fourth-down gamble that was good.

The clock had spun through more than two minutes and only 1:24 was left with the Razorbacks stationed on Texas' 39. Still too far for a field goal and still plenty of time to work it closer.

Montgomery had enjoyed a grand afternoon playing catch with Dicus, who had speared nine for 146 yards and the Porkers' second touchdown. So he zeroed in on Dicus and so did Tom Campbell.

Campbell reached the ball first, clutched it to his chest on Texas' 21 and that was the end of it.

So, as it did last year, the season ended with Texas in the Cotton Bowl and Arkansas in the Sugar. It was Arkansas's first loss in 16 games.

Until Saturday only Oklahoma had been in front of Texas, and by 14 points as Arkansas was.

The Porkers only had to move 22 yards for their first score after Bob Field picked up Koy's fumble. Montgomery passed to John Rees for 20 yards and Burnett got the last two in two bursts.

One touchdown flip to Dicus was erased by an interference penalty in the first quarter. So Texas was only seven points behind at intermission, and counting its blessings to be so close.

Arkansas had only to march 52 yards to go ahead, 14-0, with Dicus doing his duty on a 20-yard catch from Montgomery.

Then it appeared that Graham's early position on the Arkansas sideline really meant something. Even the President was stirred to comment favorably on Arkansas' quickness and Montgomery's poise.

Texas felt no compulsion to buck the Establishment, of course, or to disappoint the Rev. Graham, who was Frank Broyles' house guest and delivered the invocation.

But it was Street who had said the game would be won in the last quarter, as it had six other times since 1959.

SCORE BY QUARTERS

Texas	0	0	0	15	—	15
Arkansas	7	0	7	0	—	14

Royal huddles with Longhorn quarterback James Street.

Texas Overtakes Irish, 21-17

By Jim Trinkle
Fort Worth Star-Telegram

DALLAS, January 1, 1970

Notre Dame wasn't just kidding when it called its teams the Fighting Irish. And they don't call Texas the national champion for nothing, either.

In a finish almost too delirious for human emotions to bear, the Longhorns twice climbed off the Cotton Bowl's soggy deck Thursday to beat Notre Dame, 21-17, and defend their football crown.

Only 68 seconds were left and hardly any fingernails had survived when Texas halfback Billy Dale burst through the Irish stanchions for the winning touchdown. Dale traveled only one yard. He felt as if he had run a mile.

An overflow crowd of 73,000 and a national TV audience saw the ninth-ranked South Bend team carry the fight to the No. 1 Longhorns for the better part of the afternoon.

They broke in front by 10 points and before the day's work was done in clear, cold weather, the lead had been juggled three times.

Notre Dame led by 3-0, 10-0, and 17-14 before Texas' resourceful quarterback, James Street, marched the Horns 76 yards on the winning drive. Even then, Joe Theismann, a splendid offensive marshal for the Irish all day, had them back in Texas territory when Tom Campbell's interception smothered their last chance to knock Texas from its pedestal.

Theismann unloaded two touchdown passes — a 54-yarder to end Tom Gatewood and one to halfback Jim Yoder for 24 yards.

Scott Hempel's 26-yard field goal started Notre Dame's scoring.

As it had done all year, Texas relied on its runners. They produced in a grand fashion. Jim Bertelsen bucked a yard and Ted Koy pounded in from three yards away for the Longhorns' other touchdowns.

But for clutch running in the 34th re-run of the Dallas Classic, honors had to go to Steve Worster. The junior fullback hammered out 155 yards in 20 carries, many in third-down emergencies when Texas was fighting to extend a drive.

His total virtually matched the whole of Notre Dame's backfield, but it was Theismann's aerial wizardry that kept the Irish in position to spoil Texas' winning streak.

It was win No. 20 for the Orange, winding up a perfect schedule that began last September at California.

Texas unquestionably defended the No. 1 rank it captured when Michigan flattened Ohio State. The final poll will be counted next week.

It was a frustrating day for the slender Theismann, who moved the Irish 231 yards on his 17 pass completions. He had them on the move to the last — going from his own 23 to Texas' 39 on two passes before he let one get away. It sailed over Dennis Allan's fingers and into Tom Campbell's with 29 seconds left in the game.

As the crowd took up the chant "We're No. 1" and the scoreboard flickered "Texas — National Champions," Street took the two snapbacks and clung to the ball like it was money from home.

The game signaled Notre Dame's return to bowl contention after a 45-year absence. From the first drive you knew the Irish realized the enormity of their responsibility. Even the Vatican was listening.

So they cranked up from the opening kickoff, pounded from their 18 to Texas' 10, where Hempel was called on for a field goal. He came through from the 16 — a 26-yard effort — and even then Irish sympathizers were unfurling banners poking fun at Texas' regal standing. If the Vatican recognized the culprits, somebody's going to be excommunicated.

Having pricked the Horns with a small barb, Theismann tried to lure them to the butcher at the top of the second period. He rolled left, slipped away from his tormentors to heave a pass to Gatewood, who had sneaked behind defensive back Danny Lester, hiding his 203 pounds in the end zone — not an easy trick — until Theismann sent the ball winging to him.

So Hempel kicked the placement, it was 10-0 and Texas' crown suddenly drooped over one ear.

James Street, however, has an impediment in this logic. Not knowing he was already beaten, Street guided Texas 74 yards in nine plays, waving Bertelsen into the line for the last stride. Happy

After the game, former President Lyndon Johnson visited the Texas locker room to congratulate James Street.

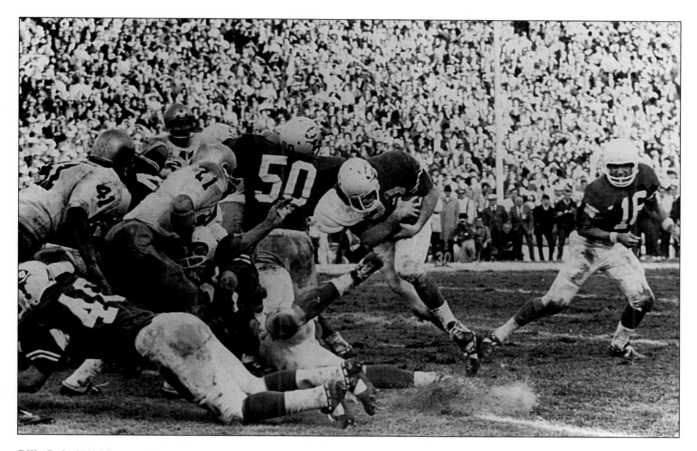

Billy Dale (23) blasts off-tackle through the stubborn Notre Dame defense.

Feller had to do it twice because of a penalty, but in time he added the point.

The 10-7 halftime count lasted through the third quarter, when Texas lost the game's only fumble.

There was a time in the second quarter when the Longhorns pushed 47 yards to Notre Dame's 7. There seemed little doubt that Feller could have tied the score with a field goal, but Darrell Royal wasn't selling short.

Nor was Bob Olson, the Irish super sophomore linebacker. He twice banged down Billy Dale to deny a first down and Notre Dame took possession on the seven.

That cinch three points that the Horns bypassed began to swell through the scoreless third period. But Street, calling on his backs for 18 straight runs, guided Texas 77 yards to score with 4:55 gone in the last quarter.

Koy whipped in from the 3, and for the first time, Texas was in front.

But not for long. Notre Dame recoiled with an 80-yard drive, with Theismann and Bill Barz doing most of the duty. At Texas' 24 Theismann got a block from Gary Kos, shucked his pursuers and threw to Yoder in the end zone. It was his first touchdown of the season.

Eight minutes separated Texas from disaster. Street passed 17 yards to Cotton Speyrer to throw the offense into gear, collected 12 from Koy, then another couple that Ted produced on a fourth-down situation. Another last-chance emergency was met when Street nailed Speyrer with a fourth-and-two dart that covered eight yards. Finally, the ball was less than a yard from the goal, and Street sent Dale skidding into the end zone for the winning points.

SCORE BY QUARTERS

Notre Dame	3	7	0	7	—	17
Texas	0	7	0	14	—	21

Horns Win in Final 12 Seconds

By Harold McKinney
Fort Worth Star-Telegram

AUSTIN, October 3, 1970

Saturday afternoon was supposed to provide the big test for Texas' secondary, but in the end it was the UCLA pass defense that flunke The Longhorns, who had been passed to the brink of disaster by Dennis Dummit, pulled out an incredible 20-17 victory on Eddie Phillips' last-minute — literally — 45-yard touchdown aerial to split end Cotton Speyrer.

The electrifying scoring bomb with only 12 seconds to play carried the No. 2-ranked Longhorns to a Southwest Conference-record 23rd straight victory and brought a capacity Memorial Stadium crowd of 65,500 to its feet cheering in a mixture of unrestrained joy and disbelief.

Until Phillips unloaded, Dummit appeared to have engineered the upset of the year.

The UCLA senior passed only sparingly — six of 10 for 140 yards — in the first half as the Longhorns rolled to a 13-3 lead at intermission.

He came out firing in the second half, however, directing scoring drives of 89 and 93 yards on the Bruins' first two possession as he riddled the Texas secondary with pin-point passes.

But it was Phillips, whose fumbles earlier had set up a UCLA field goal and killed a Texas drive at the UCLA five-yard line, who was to emerge as the hero.

The Steers, who earlier in the fourth quarter had marched from their 17 to the UCLA 13 only to give up the ball on downs, got the ball for the last time with 58 seconds to play, 49 yards from the winning touchdown.

After throwing 13 yards over the middle to Tommy Woodard for a first down at the 36, Phillips threw out of bounds to kill the clock and then fumbled out of bounds after a nine-yard loss, stopping the clock again with 33 seconds to play.

On third and 19 at the 45, Phillips sent Speyrer over the middle and hit him perfectly in full stride at the 15 between two UCLA defenders.

One, safety Doug Huff, went for the ball, unsuccessfully reaching in front of Speyrer to break up the pass. The other, Frank Jones, hung back but Speyrer simply outran him into the end zone.

Happy Feller, who kicked two field goals in the first half, including a Southwest Conference record-tying 55-yarder, followed with the extra point to put Texas ahead, 20-17, with 12 seconds left.

The Uclans had time for one more play, a long pass that Texas halfback Alan Lowry swiped — the Steers' only interception of the day.

Dummit, who broke a school record with 340 yards on 19 completions in 30 attempts, was fantastic in the second half as he chopped up the Texas defense.

Both of his touchdown passes went for 11 yards — first to split end Terry Vernoy and then to tight end Bob Christianson. The second one came at the end of a 93-yard drive

Cotton Speyrer races 45 yards for the game-winning score against UCLA.

after the Bruins had recovered Phillips' fumble at the seven.

The loss, UCLA's first after three straight victories, was even more bitter for the Bruins because early in the fourth quarter Bruce Barnes missed a 23-yard field goal attempt that would have made it 20-13.

The Bruins scored the first time they got the ball and depended on a quick, sure tackling defense to hold off the Longhorns. They held the Longhorns' rushing attack, tops in the nation with a 437.5 yards per game average, to only 235.

Steve Worster accounted for 106 yards and Jim Bertelsen added 77 for the Longhorns.

A bad pitchout by Phillips on the second play of the game helped the Bruins, 22-point underdogs, grab the 3-0 lead they held until the Longhorns finally cranked up and drove 80 yards for a touchdown in the middle of the second quarter.

Linebacker Bob Pifferini recovered Phillips' errant toss at the Texas 27-yard line and Barnes kicked his 19-yard field goal seven plays after the Bruins had driven to the Texas 2.

Linebacker Scott Henderson and tackle Scott Palmer forced UCLA to settle for the field goal by stacking up halfback Arthur Sims, the former Fort Worth Dunbar star, for a one-yard gain on a third-down and goal-to-go situation at the 3.

Feller missed 43- and 47-yard field-goal attempts on the Steers' next two possessions as the Uclan defense was able to hold in crucial situations.

The Longhorns took the lead 8:13 before intermission on Bertelsen's two-yard plunge that completed the 80-yard scoring-drive, Texas' first mistake-free series of the afternoon.

Phillips passed the Steers to the UCLA 46 and then Worster took over, blasting 33 yards and 12 yards before Bertelsen's TD.

SCORE BY QUARTERS

UCLA	3	0	14	0	—	17
Texas	0	13	0	7	—	20

Spy Thriller Ends In 6-6 Standoff

By Galyn Wilkins

Fort Worth Star-Telegram

DALLAS, October 9, 1976

Double-0-Seven would have been no help. Neither the CIA nor any other master keyhole pepper could have pulled this one out.

As James Bond once said, and as Darrell Royal and Barry Switzer were convinced Saturday afternoon, even spyglass technology never will overcome inexperienced quarterbacking in a big game.

With green skippers on both sides, Oklahoma and Texas fumbled around, hid behind conservatism and finally wandered away in a 6-6 hammerlock.

They played for the breaks, these delegates to this historic and bitter series, and they gaveth and receiveth significantly. Every point followed a drastic, abnormal event.

Texas kicked field goals after a fumble and a short punt, and Oklahoma scored a touchdown after a fumble. Texas scored a tie on the Sooners' high extra-point snap with 1:36 left in the game.

The lack of decision was a rare event in this rivalry which began at the turn of the century. The last one was in 1937, and perhaps this also will go down as one of the dullest. It simply wasn't the spontaneous combustion that normally feeds the autumnal fires of Oklahomans and Texans.

As it turned out, the blazes had been fanned by the accusation of sneaky intelligence work on the part of the OU staff by the Longhorns' coach. Royal was in a bitter and grim mood Saturday afternoon.

What was left after Royal's fusillade at Switzer was merely puffs of smoke, not an antagonistic, roaring splendid football match between offensive heavyweights. It came off not as many had hoped, but had expected.

One thing to be said for the game, the 75,000 spectators were roused by boisterous defensive play. That was, indeed, in keeping with OU-Texas tradition. The Sooners and Longhorns jerked their shirttails out, rolled up their sleeves and swung logs at each other.

"The game was exactly as I thought it would be," observed Switzer. "It was a great defensive struggle, a matter of field-position and dependence on the kicking game."

Switzer, however, also was forced to depend upon a sophomore quarterback with no more than 15 minutes varsity experience. Thomas Lott, thought Switzer, played well under the circumstances.

Lott was armed with a simple plan of off-tackle slants, a few sweeps and Lord-help-us-if-we-have-to-pass. In other words, the Wishbone's great backbreaker, the pitchout play, was used rarely and ineffectively. Lott executed only four pitches, and the Texas ends and linebackers ruined them, smashing down those four plays for a combined 19-yard loss. The Sooners were dragging with only five first downs and a mere 133 yards.

GAME 10 TEXAS VS. OKLAHOMA, 1976

President Gerald Ford joined both Royal and Barry Switzer (left) on the field prior to kickoff.

Neither could Texas sophomore Mike Cordaro fire all the spark plugs. The Longhorns generated only 182 yards and 10 first downs. Not once did they make two first downs in the same series. There wasn't the slightest hint of even a modest drive.

There was a solid feeling, even in the gut of Gerald Ford, an old Michigan center in the audience, that with Texas riding a 6-0 lead into the last six and a half minutes, OU must latch on to a miracle to win.

Deliverance for the Sooners came on an Ivy Suber fumble at the Texas 37 with 5:23 left.

Grasping their last straw, they punched home in 10 plays. Naturally they turned to the guy who destroyed the Longhorns in the fourth quarter last year, right half Horace Ivory. He gouged out 17 of those yards, including the touchdown end sweep from the one. That last short route was so uncluttered that Ivory had time to wave bye-bye to Texas defender Lionell Johnson.

Texas, on the other hand, was backed by a superior kicking game. Not merely backed, but probably saved. Russell Erxleben, the punter, booted them out of trouble at the first of the game with boots of 59, 57 and 46 yards. Russell Erxleben, the field-goal kicker, hit a 37-yard three-pointer with 20 seconds left in the first half for a 3-0 lead.

Erxleben sent a 41-yard field goal through the middle on the third play of the fourth quarter and that was the bag for the Longhorns.

"We thought we could sit back and play defense," said Royal, an angry man who was loudly jeered by the Oklahoma partisans when he emerged from the tunnel into the jeweled sunlight. "We played defense for 60 minutes I thought. We fought like hell and I don't feel we won."

SCORE BY QUARTERS

Texas	0	3	0	3	—	6
Oklahoma	0	0	0	6	—	6

Switzer Says 'Spy' Ordeal Over

By Jim Reeves and Dick Moore

Fort Worth Star-Telegram

Oklahoma coach Barry Switzer didn't mince words.

"Fellas," he said as the press gathered round following Saturday's 6-6 tie with Texas in the Cotton Bowl, "we're here to talk about the football game. That's it, understand."

It wasn't a question more like a declaration of the way things would be.

What Switzer didn't want to discuss was the alleged "spy incident" which grabbed headlines after Texas coach Darrell Royal leveled accusations at Switzer, OU defensive coach Larry Lacewell and an Oklahoma businessman Friday.

Relations were strained between the two head coaches Saturday. They did not speak before the game, not even when meeting and walking out to midfield with President Ford. Nor did they greet each other after the game.

"It's over now," said Switzer. "I made my statements on the matter yesterday (Friday). I don't care what he (Royal) thinks."

Switzer admitted he did not seek Royal out before the game, as has been the custom of the two head coaches in past contests.

But the OU boss did walk toward the center of the field when the game ended, apparently to meet with Royal as is customary.

"I went out to the middle of the field looking for him," said Switzer. "I was going to wave at him but I never saw him. If Texas had won the game, I definitely would have gone over to congratulate him."

Switzer said the two head coaches did not speak with each other as they walked out with Ford for the pre-game coin flip.

"I'd have to say the President, and the Secret Service, were in complete command," Switzer said. "We didn't have a chance to say much of anything."

Lacewell, a close friend of Lonnie Williams, the alleged OU "spy," said he'd like to see the matter ended.

"I didn't spy and that's the end of it," said Lacewell. "You get calls from people all the time. I don't have time for that bleep. I've got coaching to do."

Lacewell said he is a close friend of Williams and that the two converse frequently, including this past week. "But Lonnie and I did not talk football this week."

Lacewell said he did not meet Royal's challenge for a lie detector test.

"I'm not going to take a lie detector test," said Lacewell emphatically. "I'm not gonna run down here answering to Royal every time he gets mad.

"If he has any facts of wrongdoing, let him present them to the NCAA, and I'm sure they'll act on them," Lacewell said. "Besides, if lie detector tests aren't good enough for the courts, they're not good enough for me."

Royal said he could only guess what might happen next.

BIOGRAPHIES

ABOUT THE AUTHOR

Mike Jones has been a sportswriter with the *Fort Worth Star-Telegram* since 1983, where he has covered the Southwest Conference and the Big 12 Conference.

Previously, he covered the Southwest Conference, the Dallas Cowboys and the Texas Rangers for *The Dallas Morning News* from 1968 to 1981.

A native of Kilgore, Tex., this is his first book.

ABOUT THE EDITOR

Dan Jenkins is one of America's most renowned sports writers. Jenkins is the author of more than a dozen books, including the bestsellers, *Semi-Tough* (1972), *Dead Solid Perfect* (1974), *Limo* (1976), *Baja Oklahoma* (1981), *Life It's Own Self* (1984), *Fast Copy* (1988), and *You Gotta Play Hurt* (1991).

A native of Fort Worth and an alumnus of TCU, Jenkins' most enjoyable boyhood memories are having watched Sam Baugh and Davey O'Brien lead the Horned Frogs to national championships in 1935 and 1938.